Matter and Mokṣa

Matter and Mokṣa

Science and Spirituality in Jainism

Medhavi Jain

With a Foreword by
Shugan Chand Jain

DK PRINTWORLD
Publishers of Indian Traditions

Cataloging in Publication Data — DK
[Courtesy: D.K. Agencies (P) Ltd. <docinfo@dkagencies.com>]

Jain, Medhavi, 1977- **author.**
Matter and mokṣa : science and spirituality in Jainism / Medhavi Jain ; with a foreword by Shugan Chand Jain.
pages cm
Includes bibliographical references.
ISBN 9788124612170

1. Jainism and science. 2. Mokṣa. 3. Matter – Religious aspects – Jainism. 4. Jaina philosophy. I. Title.

LCC BL1375.S35J35 2025 | DDC 294.4165 23

ISBN 978-81-246-1217-0
First Published in 2025

Printed and published by:
D.K. Printworld (P) Ltd.
Regd. Office: "Vedaśrī", F-395 Sudershan Park
(Metro Station: ESI Hospital), New Delhi - 110015
Phones: (011) 4172 2626, 98713 94815
e-mail: indology@dkprintworld.com
Web: www.dkprintworld.com

Dedicated to
an esteemed scholar
who showed me the way to
wisdom pursuit

Late **Acharya Gopi Lal Amar Ji**
(19 October 1935 – 8 July 2014)

Foreword

I COMPLIMENT Dr Medhavi Jain for selecting an appropriate topic for her first scholarly endeavour, which is the need of the hour. In Jainism, we find two active substances opposite in nature, viz. *jīva* (consciousness), which is non-concrete, and *pudgala* (matter), whose nature is fusion and fission, and which is concrete, i.e. cognizable by sensory perception. Whatever we see and observe in the universe results from the interaction between these two substances. In this context, science and spirituality are the two main subjects. Where science enquires about the matter (*pudgala*), spirituality deals with the soul (*jīva*).

Jaina philosophy deals with both these subjects uniquely as it conveys that matter attracts and, in turn, attracted by the *jīva* affecting its actions and experiences of pain and pleasure. The *jīva* is the pure soul, bound by material bodies like emotions and beliefs, *karma* and the physical body, which give different identities and cause each living being different experiences of pain and pleasure. It is the quality of matter which makes the *jīva* forget its nature of infinite perception, knowledge, energy and bliss, resulting in its attachment to it and causing it to develop emotions of anger, aversion and greed resulting in pain.

Mokṣa (liberation), or the state of bliss, implies the state of pure soul free from all forms of material bondage and enjoys its fourfold nature of infinity. According to Jainism, this is the ideal that each living being wishes to attain by trying to develop total detachment/ dissociation from matter.

The curious ones amongst us initiate a process to enquire about happy and unhappy experiences, and learn what real happiness is. Being inquisitive, Dr Jain is on her way to decode the fundamental nature of things. She starts this process to understand the Jaina doctrine, enquiring about *karma* and its relationship with the soul and eventually covers liberation. She simultaneously validates her findings with the results of research in science, psychology, philosophical and wellness-enhancing literature, and experiences of well-known personalities. I wish her good luck on this path.

Shugan C. Jain
President, ISJS

Preface

INDIA has always been the spiritual leader of the world, as it is the birthplace of the four most ancient religious philosophies: Jainism, the Vedas, Yoga and Buddhism. Though all religions of the world indicate the essence of the same universal reality, there are different approaches to accessing that. And that, too, to a certain extent only, as truth is a matter of realization and irrespective of how many scriptures are penned down to make mankind understand the path towards reality, they are only helpful if one dives into the essence of their subject matter.

In that context, philosophy of Jainism depicts the whole evolutionary journey of an individual soul, right from when it is a unicellular being struggling in the lowest dimensions of the cosmos to the most developed human, who stands at the pinnacle of evolution. One needs to be corrected if one thinks that evolution ends with becoming human, as the Jaina philosophy depicts that only humans are equipped with the natural ability to understand the ultimate purpose of everything in the world; hence, being human is a far greater responsibility.

Attaining the human body is the pinnacle of physical evolution, with the most developed organs, especially the brain. What comes next is the apex of spiritual evolution. Spiritual evolution here means stepping out of the beginningless cycle of cause and effect, and attaining the purest state of the soul with absolutely no kārmic baggage. And when there is no baggage at all, the soul is free in the real sense, and this state is known as liberation (*mokṣa*).

Breaking down all that exists reveals two substances: matter, which belongs to the physical world, and the soul, the abstract entity behind the activities of matter. Where the absolute matter is the *paramāṇu*, the absolute soul is the *paramātmā*.

However, I do not know how big a thing I am talking about. I can only say, as a beginner, that this work of mine is just a baby step into the ocean of India's immense treasure of wisdom. It will give the readers an overall understanding of the philosophy of Jainism. Let me admit that this work is for my clarification first and the readers come second.

Upbringing in a multicultural atmosphere by a Gupta father and a Punjabi mom gave me a broader perspective on how to observe life. I got to study in a Sikh school, too, for two years, and I had friends from all communities in my childhood. This resulted in an opening that could accept people of different religious perspectives and their points of view; it also helped me develop better emotional intelligence. Gladly, this scenario continued when I got married into a Jaina family. Little did I know that my spiritual transformation would be caused by studying this ancient Indian philosophy. Even little did I know that one day, I would be on the path of becoming a scholar of the same.

15 November 2024
Guru Nanak Jayanti

Medhavi Jain

Acknowledgements

Expressing gratitude through words cannot do justice to what our forebearers have done for us in the process of moulding their path.

I BOW to our family *guru*, honorary late Ācārya Bāhubali jī Mahārāj. I pay my respectful homage to his disciple, the late Āryikā Śrut Devī Mātā jī, who led me to study the philosophical teachings of the great Indian soul scientists under her guidance.

Heartfelt reverence to the late scholar Ācārya Gopi Lal Amar jī, who motivated me to pursue an academic career.

Thanks and gratitude are due to the honorary scholar of Vedic and Jaina studies, Professor Dayanand Bhargava, for constantly showering his blessings upon me and showing me the right path.

Sincere gratitude to respected Professor Anekant Kumar Jain, Professor and Head, Department of Jain Philosophy, Faculty of Philosophy, Sri Lal Bahadur Shastri Rashtriya Sanskrit Vidyapeeth, New Delhi, for being a problem solver and a torch-bearer to me.

I thank my friend Dr Natalia Zhelznova, a Russian scholar of the philosophy of Jainism. Natalia not only gave me some excellent suggestions on how to write a good scholarly book but also cleared some of my doubts and influenced my mind how to do critical thinking.

I thank Dr Robert Zydenbos, the Dutch – Canadian scholar of Jainism, who not only shared some of his insights about different aspects of Jainism with me through email but also sent me the PDF version of his incredible book *Jainism Today and Its Future* (2006).

I would like to express my heartfelt gratitude to Dr Narender Bhandari, India's space scientist and a scholar of Jainism, for helping me immensely with the chapters of Science and Anekāntavāda. As per Dr Bhandari's suggestions, I made a few changes even in the references given from other books.

I am grateful to Dr Ashok Kumar Jain, the renowned Indian physicist and the retired head of the Department of Physics at IIT Roorkee. Discussions with him were eye-opening during my research journey.

Sincere gratitude to Dr Shugan Chand Jain, Founder of the International School of Jain Studies (ISJS), for always giving the right advice and writing the Foreword for this work.

My special thanks and gratitude go to Dr Rekha Jain, a former economics professor at the University of Delhi, for not only pushing me to send this book for publishing but also motivating me continuously to be confident about its content quality. This book would not have been possible without her persistence.

My heartfelt respect and gratitude goes to my virtual friend and uncle, Mr Late Chandramohan Shah, whom I have never met but who showed confidence in me through my social media posts and guided me in the best way possible. He also introduced me to the incredible artist Mrs Kavita Shah, whose artwork can be seen on the cover page of this work — a huge thanks to her for gifting her exemplary painting.

I want to thank Mr Susheel Mittal, Director of D.K. Printworld, for providing valuable feedback on improving this work. After meeting him personally, I realized how challenging the publisher's task is.

I want to express my gratitude to my husband, Mr Parveen Jain (CMD, Tulip Group), and my children, Divyanshi and Siddharth, for respecting and valuing my dreams of spreading this beautiful Indian philosophy. I also want to thank my mother, Mrs Shashi Gupta, for having immense faith in me and for feeling on cloud nine upon each of my achievements. Thanks a ton to my father, Mr Bimal Gupta, for being silently proud of me.

Contents

1

Main Theories and Practices in Jainism

Right Conduct and Ethics

> *An ethic is the intrinsic choice of the consciousness between universal right and wrong, of which it naturally chooses the universal right while in its pure or less infected state.*

THE modern definitions of conduct and ethics are "to cause (oneself) to act or behave in a particular and especially in a controlled manner"[1] and "the discipline concerned with what is morally good and bad, and morally right and wrong"[2] respectively.The Indian philosophers describe everything in the context of the evolution of consciousness which occurs when the soul is in sync with the functioning of the universe. Hence, right knowledge and right world view have been emphasized as essentials to understand the right conduct. An eminent scholar Jinendra Varni defines *cāritra* (conduct or the right way to lead life) as "(right) conduct is through which benevolence (of the soul) is achieved and harm is deterred" (2014a: 282) and *ācāra* (ethics) has been defined as "according to

---

1 "Conduct", Merriam-Webster.com. Merriam-Webster, 2022 (accessed on 19 September 2022). www.merriam-webster.com/dictionary/conduct.

2 "Ethics", Britannica.com. Britannica, 2020 (accessed on 11 January 2021). www.britannica.com/topic/ethics-philosophy.

one's willpower the efforts made to enhance one's enlightened world view" (Varni 2012: 240). We see that in the definition of ethics the scholar clarifies the importance of one's free will, which is neither influenced by someone nor has been originated from an outer influence. This way an ethic becomes an innate choice of an individual that eventually motivates one to adopt the right conduct.

In the philosophy of Jainism, right conduct has been described for two categories of truth seekers: one is for the laymen and the other for the ascetics. For laymen, it is mild, whereas for the ascetics, it is of high order. In the text, about how a householder's conduct should be, Ācārya Samantabhadra writes:[3]

> True knowledge knows the practice of the examination of behaviour as pertaining to the rise, growth and preservation of (good) conduct of householders and houseless renouncers.

Hence, the importance of right knowledge has also been conveyed by the teachers in order to adopt the right ethics and, through them, to follow the right conduct.

In the text on reality, Ācārya Umāsvāti[4] mentions, "abstinence from violence, falsehood, stealing, carnality and possessiveness — these are the vows" (Tatia 2011: 169) and in the very next *sūtra* of the same text, the teacher clarifies the differentiation of the same vows for householders and for the saints,[5] "partial abstinence is a small vow and complete abstinence is a great vow" (ibid.: 170). For a saint, these practices are the toughest and hence are called *mahāvrata* (great vows), whereas for a layman, they are comparatively easier and are called *aṇuvrata* (minor vows). Each thought that gets originated in one's mind, each word one utters and each action one

---

3 *gṛhamedhyanagārāṇāṁ cāritrotpatti vṛddhirakṣāṅgam* ।
caraṇānuyogasamayaṁ samyagjñānaṁ vijānāti ॥
— *Ratnakaraṇḍakaśrāvakācāra* 45

4 *hiṁsāva-tasteyābrahmaparigrahebhyo viratirvratama* ।
— *Tattvārthasūtra* 7.1

5 *deśasarvato 'ṇumahatī* । — Ibid. 7.2

performs have to be checked in order to avoid violence of any kind, to any living being and to be in harmony with the nature, with the whole universe. We notice that lying, stealing, promiscuousness and mindless hoarding of objects, these four are types of violence only. Hence, we analyse that the first and foremost vow is non-violence which acts as a foundation for the rest of the four. This is the reason why *ahiṁsā* (non-violence) has been propagated in this philosophy as the most important principle.

Depicting the control of an ascetics' mind, Ācārya Umāsvāti writes in *Tattvārthasūtra:*[6]

> Controlling speech, controlling the mind, moving about carefully, handling implements carefully, inspecting food and drink properly to ensure they are acceptable. — Tatia 2011: 170

These actions strengthen the vow of non-violence; even for householders, the same advice applies though with milder striction. Just like the leader of a family or a nation is expected to be the most responsible. Humans, being able to stand at the pinnacle of the evolutionary ladder, are supposed to be the most responsible and answerable towards their role of the leader of earth. In terms of taking care of the natural resources, it can be the conservation of nature or animals. Hence, in the context of right eating choices "the Jains expect much more from human beings than convenient easy slaughter" (Tobias 1991: 17). As each being on the planet has the basic right to live, Jainism tells us to be self-interrogatory by simply conveying "perform every action mindfully" and eating choices come first in this category of mindfulness.

> The Jains say that no individual should interfere in another's life; that absolute non-interference is the beginning of compassion.
> — Ibid. 36

6 *vāṅ-manogupti-ryā-dānanikṣepaṇasamityālokitapānabhojanāni pāñca* ।
— *Tattvārthasūtra* 7.4

The first step has to be taken by a person for oneself. One cannot do much about the cruelty occurring around the world, however, one can cultivate one's inner realms through wilfully scrutinizing each of her/his actions.

India has taught the lessons of *ahiṁsā* to the world. We all praise the persona of Mahatma Gandhi for his non-violent ways in dealing with even the most significant political decisions of his life. World's great personalities like "Albert Einstein, George Bernard Shaw, Martin Luther King Jr and Nelson Mandela" (Malhotra 2015) are amongst the few global personalities who were highly influenced by Gandhi's belief in non-violence and always used it for sustaining peace. But rarely people know about the root of Gandhi's faith in non-violence. Impact from one's childhood stays with one for the whole life and keeps reflecting in each of one's doings. Gandhiji's close friendship with Raychandbhai Mehta, who became famous as the spiritual teacher Shrimad Rajchandra later, had an immense influence on Gandhi. He spent around twenty years of his youth at a communal house in Ahmedabad. During those years, the concept of *ahiṁsā* as the true religion got inculcated deeply in his persona. "Gandhi was to show how *ahiṁsā* could work on the level of an entire nation in the twentieth century" (Tobias 1991: 102). Not only *ahiṁsā* but also concepts like the importance of self-restraint as an integral part of life and the significance of truth in all personal and professional dealings were emphasized by him. These traits are seen as universal laws and are deeply practised by the Jaina laymen.

India has volumes of history of not only the enlightened saints but also of the powerful kings who ruled their kingdoms non-violently. "Khārvela was a Jaina king of Kaliṅga in the present-day Odisha, who ruled during the second or first century BCE."[7]

> It is significant that there is no mention of his having ever killed an enemy. The conqueror used benign means, apparently, to force

---

[7] <https://en.wikipedia.org/wiki/Kharavela> "Kharvela", 4 September 2022 (accessed on 6 September 2022).

> the will of his opponents and eventually devoted all of his time to serving Jain monks. — Tobias 1991: 100

One may find Jaina philosophy as the philosophy of self-introspection, where there is no finger raised towards any other, but within. There is no God, but within; no desire of improvement of others, but of the self; no outward travelling, but within.

> *O human! identify thyself with your real essence and not with what your circumstances modify you into.*

Mostly we consider our home, relationships, property and jewellery as our possessions. If one has a philosophical bent of mind, one considers one's body as a possession too. However, ancient Jaina philosophers were far ahead and declared one's emotions as one's possessions too. Even one's gender is considered as an inner possession. Jinendra Varni defines *parigraha* as:

> Possessions are of two types – inner and outer. The *rāga* (emotions) of the *jīva* is inner possession and due to these emotions, incessant assumption and accumulation of outer objects by the affected person is outer possession. At the base of each outer possession lies the root of inner passion/emotion, hence inner possession is considered as the main. — Varni 2014b: 23

Thinkers of Jaina philosophy have described fourteen inner possessions we identify as us. At any given time, each of us possesses twelve of them, excluding the two genders. These inner possessions are termed psychic dispositions of the soul. They are:

> *Mithyātva* (wrong-belief), *krodha* (anger), *māna* (pride), *māyā* (delusion), *lobha* (greed), *hāsya* (laughter), *rati* (copulation), *arati* (abstinence), *śoka* (mourning), *bhaya* (fear), *jugupsā* (hatred), *strīveda* (female gender), *puruṣaveda* (male gender) and *napuṁsaka veda* (neuter gender). — Ibid. 2014a: 273

While the efficient control of these psychic dispositions is necessary to ascend the spiritual ladder, it is an innate part of the conduct because uncontrolled emotions lead to uncontrolled violence. Untamed inner possessions lead to unbound material possessions.

"In Jainism, ethics is the first and foremost matter of personal responsibility" (Zydenbos 2006: 58), where one is answerable to none other than the self; even one's family, society and nation come afterward.

> A strong sense of individual responsibility that forces everyone to consciously think over one's actions and attitudes. — Ibid.

Especially nowadays, when one is under the constant influence of misinformation spread through different mass media platforms, news that propagates religious intolerance and hatred, even in the context of one's diet, ethics in Jaina philosophy continuously motivate one to have one's own thoughts and choices in each matter. The purpose of being mindful at all times leads to improvising the self and to accept others as they are. The effort to lessen or eliminate one's own imperfections leads one to climb the ladder of spiritual evolution.

Non-violence is our innate nature; one's desire of being ethical is not, and can never be, a forced phenomenon but one's innate desire to return to one's true nature that is morally elated and joyful. Every person around the world focuses on being happy, each philosophy emphasizes that inner happiness cannot be achieved by material possessions. "Happiness is self-contained and self-sufficient. Happy men are free men" (Rand 1952: 636) for they are not only in sync with their inner selves but also with the laws of the universe. Indeed true happiness is freedom because it is ethical and comes from the feeling that none of one's actions or achievements is causing harm to any being by any means.

In his book *Messages from the Masters*, Brian Weiss (2000: 10) calls the deities as masters. He writes:

> The messages from the Masters remind us to allow our minds to return to what is important and to put aside what is unimportant.

When consumerism is winning over the masses' brains through all ethical and unethical means, so much so that everybody is under the influence of what to eat, what to buy, what to wear, whom to follow, how to look and so on. Ethics, as described in this Indian philosophy, help us tremendously in not only choosing the products we use wisely and thoughtfully but also in developing our own individual thinking.

Often in our normal life, we tend to judge even our close relationships; we are not aware if this judgement does any harm to others but it surely harms us. Hence, becoming non-judgemental comes under ethics too; for it prevents us from being violent to our inner selves by having harmful thoughts. The whole purpose of gaining knowledge and being spiritual is that one starts the journey within. "Jain culture discourages judgement of others and encourages self-criticism" (Mardia and Rankin 2013: 16). Though the beauty of this statement has been lost today, this is the most wonderful aspect of Jaina philosophy as self-introspection has the ability to take one towards salvation. *Ahiṁsā* is a universal law.

> *Ahiṁsā* means non-interference with the natural balance and allowing every aspect of life and nature its own place and dignity.
>
> — Ibid.: 2

In the present-day scenario when *Homo sapiens* has crossed all boundaries of giving personal space to the elements of nature, be it domesticated and wild animals or forests, mountains, water resources, land, etc. we must contemplate on returning to simplicity. In the quest of fulfilling his blind, self-oriented desires, man today has become a monster. He has moulded the planet in a way where only he exists and only his wishes and necessities matter. No other being has even the basic right of life if man does not want it. Whereas

> even life forms invisible to the naked eye can be highly complex systems that play an unseen but critical role in sustaining life in its entirety.
>
> — Ibid.: 9

Unicellular bacteria also have the ability to help humans to sustain their health along with causing chaos. Recent encounters with the Corona virus have shaken up the world immensely, where packets of genetic matter caused havoc, which resulted in the loss of millions of lives. As a matter of fact, these unicellular bacteria and viruses, too, have a significant role in the cosmos.

The research about the important role of tiny organisms in sustaining the planet's environmental health by environmentalists may be a newly-found phenomenon which oozed out from the threat of global warming and the harm the human race is causing to mother earth. However, "for a Jain ascetic, this would be no surprise, but an expression of the obvious" (Mardia and Rankin 2013: 9). For the knowers of this philosophy, respect for each life form falls within the ambit of right conduct, and one's unawareness about the same is considered as ignorance. In his book *Life Force: The World of Jainism*, Michael Tobias writes:

> You cannot save the world, but you can cultivate your own garden, which the Jains know to be the soul. — 1991: 7

There can never be the question of superiority of one over the other, at least in terms of their right to live. The difference lies not in souls but in the rung on the ladder of evolution, where each being is located at present, as all souls share the same attribute of knowing and perceiving. It may sound like an imaginary state of perfectionism, but for Jainas, it is an inbred thought they grow up with. Those who are aware of the teachings of this philosophy understand the seriousness of causing cruelty to any being under any circumstance. Violation of this causes serious repercussions that affect their journey of evolution and result in birth in hellish dimensions, and the journey to step out of the cycle of cause and effect becomes even lengthier. As the most developed species, it is necessary not to violate the fundamental right to live of every being and to strive to save whenever any organism can be saved.

> Without extending that hand of freedom to every other organism, there is no solace, can be no moment's respite. —Tobias 1991: 7

The way one has the right to live, so does every other being, as we share the same life force.

When a housefly troubles one during one's chores, one keeps shooing it away, and it keeps coming back with even more intensity to trouble one. One often thinks, why the heck does it not understand? Philosophers can ponder that the fly has a lesser sense of scrutinizing its behaviour. As humans, we stand at the pinnacle of contemplating from the simplest to the most complicated matters, and not only to judge each situation wisely but also to choose what is better for us to ascend the ladder of physical and spiritual evolution further. Hence, "as a species capable of profound introspection, we should have outgrown the carnivore mentality" (ibid.: 11).

This is why the journey to make the world a better place starts with oneself, including respect towards each living organism. Seeing the present exploitation of natural resources causing havoc already, majority of the people on the planet need to rethink their eating habits. For example, is it really required to get nutrition from animal protein? Is it really essential for good health and a fulfilling life? Because nature has plenty of examples of gigantic animals who, despite being their mammoth size, are vegetarians.

> Contrary to evolutionary expectation, the elephant, the gorilla, the rhino, the hippo, are all vegetarians, in spite of the human presumption that the mighty need meat. — Ibid.: 12

By 2010, an immense boost in animal agriculture indicated that

> livestock systems occupy about 30 per cent of the planet's ice-free terrestrial surface area and are a significant global asset with a value of at least $1.4 million. — Thornton 2010

It would be futile to clarify further why it becomes necessary for the governments to condition people's minds that eating meat is the right and healthier option. In a world where ethics are considered apt only when dealing with humans, this Indian philosophy uniquely conveys the essence and individuality of each life-force, each soul.

Whenever one is upset with negative thoughts and emotions, one is suggested to be a spectator of them as they are temporary in nature and eventually go their own way. Similarly, when it comes to, be it craving for food or an intense feeling to let out anger at someone or any other emotion that makes a human take a mindless decision. One is advised to be an observer, as even these pass by soon. Tobias writes:

> Those "few minutes" of psychological impasse, passion, disinterest, oblivion, appetite are the same few moments that it takes to vent rage, to murder someone, to inflict every pain known to the human arsenal. – 1991: 13

These few moments, if not controlled, cause tiny, individual damages like obesity and other diseases, and more extensive havoc like world wars, mass killings and division of nations, to name a few.

People have caused most of the chaos around the world, in the name of God, where "in the last thousand years about 40 million people have died in the name of religion" (Mallo 2015). Amidst this destruction, this Indian philosophy conveys a unique message as "Jainism is the only religion that has no God, and yet is not atheistic" (Tobias 1991: 15). It states that there is no God who is the doer of our fate; rather, he is the one who has broken the shackles of *karma* and has achieved *mokṣa* (Godhood or liberation) and, in the process, has shown us the way to walk on that path.

"Return to Innocence" is a 1994 song by Enigma Greman musical group. It is about returning to one's nature and not letting one's mind be influenced by society. Beautifully, Jainism talks about it at all times.

> What has stood out in Jainism for me is its penetrating insights, phenomenal integrity and childlike idealism — unblushing,

> naked, powerful and enduring. It is like a telegram from the earth itself.
> — Tobias 1991: 17

Jainism lays the ground for a world where every human is filled with exaltation and lives compassionately and fearlessly, for he exists in absolute sync with the universe.

Being the most developed species on the planet, the universe expects more from us. We are the caretakers of the earth's resources and must enact in that way. "Art" is one way to express this responsibility. Touching the essence of human achievements, Tobias writes, "our art is flourishing, not because we have killed, but because we have loved" (ibid.: 14). No matter how disturbed we are, art can save us from destruction, taking us into the realm of ingenuity. We find solace as "imagination realigns the soul" (ibid.: 15). In the process of creation, an artist travels to the innermost, the unconditional, the benevolent realms of the consciousness that help her in dealing with the garbage of conscious as well as subconscious mind creatively. Art plays a vital role in keeping this most developed species sane. Any form of art, be it writing, painting, acting, dancing or sports; or any other specific skill to create something, has the ability to save us from destruction, for it transforms the inner darkness into illuminating light. The famous Spanish artist Pablo Picasso (1881–1973) gave many quotes about how art is able to deal with the same. Two of his quotes are worth mentioning in this context, "art is the elimination of the unnecessary" and "the purpose of art is washing the dust of daily life off our souls".[8]

Nations are working towards making themselves equipped with all kinds of weapons, be they atomic, bio or chemical. Ethical teachings of Jainism can guide the human race, for violence can never be the quest for the true nature of consciousness.

---

[8] Famous Pablo Picasso Quotes. Pablopicasso.org. Pablo Picasso 2022, <https://www.pablopicasso.org/quotes.jsp> (accessed on 23 September 2022).

Karma in Jaina Philosophy

The idea that somebody higher out there is sitting with enormous record books, monitoring everyone's *karma*, boggles each psyche. When one acknowledges that the universe is keeping this record inevitably, the principle of *karma* begins to open in front of one.

Understanding *karma* profoundly implies that one is ready to take the absolute liability of one's activities; without interference from some supernatural being, and wonderfully this is but an opportunity to take the command of one's life in own hands. How can it be believed that a significantly positioned authority is either able to or allowed to give results of *karma* executed by someone else? For what reason would anybody, be it God, does as such? Why would they invest much energy in ascertaining another person's *karma*? How many employees must employ to dreadful keep track of each being's past, present and future *karmas*? Who chooses which accolade or punishment to be given for every great or deed of one? There might be *karma* of various sorts, some may bring fruits in a lesser time, and others may require long efforts to get the results. Who decides when and how much fruit to give somebody for a specific *karma* one has performed?

All of us have heard about the law of attraction, which conveys: "Positive thoughts bring positive results into a person's life, while negative thoughts bring negative outcomes" (Scott 2020). It is like — each of us works like an antenna that continuously sends signals into the cosmos, signals which eventually not only manifest themselves in physical form but also return to the same person who emitted them. Whereas good signals bring goodness in life, the negative ones get negativity. But, is the *karma* principle that simple? Jaina philosophy goes into the subtlest of this theory and decodes it to the core.

We observe that most people talk about *karma*, where almost everyone has this basic understanding of Isaac Newton's Third Law of Motion, which says — for every action, there is an equal and opposite reaction. However, Jainism describes the same law with the highest grade of subtlety and majorly divides *karma* into two categories — *dravya karma,* which is a "special kind of *pudgala skandha* (material particles)" (Varni 2014a: 25), and *bhāva karma* (the psychic dispositions of the soul), that is "binding of *dravya karma* through the subtle activities of mind, speech and actions" (ibid.). Together, both of these act in the following way:

> Through the influence of *bhāva karma* certain minute, elementary, material groups of particles enter into the space points of the soul and get bound with it. — Ibid.

The soul and the *karma* start sharing the same space, like milk mixed with water.

This is the law of nature, the same for every being, regardless of its location in the universe, irrespective of how underdeveloped it is. Thinking about how the universe would react to our wrongdoings is interesting. Be it uttering a lie, stealing something or engaging in anything more violent, like killing. In Jainism, there is absolutely no involvement of a judge. Hence, stealing at present means attracting the shortcoming of that specific object in future for the one who steals. Similarly, causing pain to someone attracts pain to the one who caused it in the first place. These are but the simple yet profound laws of nature.

> The Jainas believe that there is an innate moral order to the cosmos, self-regulating through the workings of *karma*.
>
> — Zydenbos 2006: 20

When it comes to man-made laws, it happens around us that people escape their punishments by using their wealth or political influence. Does that mean they get saved from that crime? In the context of the *karma* theory, it is an obvious "no", for sooner or later, the one who has violated the law has to go through the repercussions of the violence he caused to the other being. In India, there is a saying — God's stick does not make voice. Jaina philosophy replaces the word God with the universe, which enacts a mirror that reflects what is being kept in front of it.

Each of us consistently performs *karma*, knowingly or unknowingly, breathing, sitting, dozing and eating; each activity falls under the ambit of *karma*. The joy, hardships, possessions, mental peace, well-being, and anything, even the body we dwell in, are because of our previously bonded *karma*. Jaina psychology and meṭaphysics focus on the relation between the self and the non-self. Each movement created by the consciousness, be it physical, vocal or mental, is depicted as a sort of vibration "by which an interaction with *ajīva*, all that is the non-self, takes place" (Zydenbos 2006: 37).

Ācārya Umāsvāti mentions in his *Tattvārthasūtra*,[9] the operation of the body, speech and mind is action" (Tatia 2011: 151). When one is sleeping, despite not performing a task, he is performing the action of sleep. Each type of activity, be it physical, mental, even emotional, subtle or gross, can be defined as *karma*.

> The term *karma* denotes the subtle aggregates of the kārmic matter, which are attracted and assimilated by the soul.
>
> — Tater 2009: Preface

Consistently, the degrees of all *karma*s keep fluctuating according to a being's vibrations.

Cause and Aspects of Kārmic Bondage

Tattvārthasūtra 6.2 (*sa āsravaha*) depicts that "the threefold action is the cause of the inflow of *karma*" (Tatia 2011: 151). Together, actions of the mind, words and body are called *yoga*, which causes the incessant inflow of *karma*.

We often feel that joyous times get spent as lighter as flowers, whereas the tragic period seems as if they take ages. We observe that whenever we are happy, we feel elated and ready to do whatever we have planned. While bad moods or woeful times make us feel

---

9 *kāyāvān-manaḥkarma yogaḥ* । — *Tattvārthasūtra* 6.1

heavier in mind, which results in bad performance overall. That eventually enacts as the cause to bind not-so-good *karma* for us.

Analysing both events under the microscope of *karma*, one finds that sorrow indicates heavier kārmic particles; however, happiness appears to have a lighter weightage of *karma*. In happier times, one is more inclined to be in touch with one's true nature, which is peaceful and compassionate. In contrast, bad times increase the chances of identifying the self (pure consciousness) with the non-self (inanimate kārmic matter). Hence, grief increases the chances of bondage into the world. However, the Jaina thinkers have described that happiness and sorrow are the causes of "the bondage of the self in *saṁsāra*, the cycle of recurring rebirths" (Zydenbos 2006: 38). And the theory of *karma* depicts that one needs to step out of not only bad but also good to attain liberation.

In the text on reality, Ācārya Umāsvāti states:[10]

> There are four aspects of bondage: type, duration, intensity (quality) of fruition and mass of the material particles assimilated.
>
> — Tatia 2011: 191

We notice that the results of *karma* are not something given by some superior, divine power but are natural laws which depend on a few factors, like with which intensity a specific *karma* has been performed, whether the intent was good, medium, bad or amongst any of the varied degrees. This, in turn, decides the type of bondage and duration of the fruition of that particular *karma*. Beautifully, each of these happens rationally, in the form of aggregation of material particles.

Types of Karma

Each *karma* is like a force that obligates the soul to undergo the effect of its actions when that particular activity takes place. Just as the quality of a seed depicts the tree's health in the future, the intensity of *karma* performed expresses the nature, type

---

[10] *prakṛti-sthity-anubhāva-pradeśās-tadvidhāyāḥ* । — *Tattvārthasūtra* 8.4

and duration of the same in future at the very specific time that particular *karma* is executed.

Ācārya Umāsvāti describes:[11]

> There are eight principal types of kārmic bondage: knowledge-covering, intuition-covering, sensation, deluding, lifespan, body, status and obstructive. — Tatia 2011: 191

Examples of these *karma*s can be observed in our surroundings, though the degrees may vary. For example, going to school or college for a degree can be the simplest example of a step towards peeling the knowledge-obscuring *karma*. However, in the context of knowledge, it is much higher and refers to the direct knowledge (*pratyakṣa-jñāna*), the first step of which begins with realizing the self.

Similarly, the example of intuition-covering *karma* can be felt by getting a clearer perception of events, objects and people. Sensation *karma* occurs in the feelings of a healthier body or pain in any part of the body. Deluding *karma* is the most dangerous of all *karma*s as it does not let the veil of ignorance get lifted due to the irrational affection of the soul towards any of the relationships, objects, etc. Lifespan *karma* is the specific age one lives for; body-making *karma* decides if the being will have a healthier or defective body. Status *karma* determines the family one takes birth in, and obstructive *karma* either removes the interruptions on one's way towards knowledge, realization, etc., or enhances them.

Interestingly, the eight types of *karma* can be further grouped into two: one category belongs to those which have negative effects on the soul and at the same time, the soul can shed them with its efforts, known as *ghātī karma*, viz. knowledge-obstructing (*jñānāvaraṇīya*), perception-covering (*darśanāvaraṇīya*), delusion (*mohanīya*) and obstructive (*antarāya*) *karmas*. Whereas, the second category has the rest four, which are once bound, will only be shed

11 *ādyā jñāna darśanāvaraṇa vedanīya mohanīyā yuṣka nāma gotrā antarāyāḥ* ı — *Tattvārthasūtra* 8.5

when their time is complete. At the same time, these do not affect the workings of the soul. They are known as *aghātī karmas*; in this group we have age (*āyu*), body-making (*nāma karma*), societal status (*gotra*) and feeling of affliction (*vedanīya*) *karmas*.

> The *aghātī karmas* determine the longevity, the personal appearance, the social circumstances and sensitivity to pleasure and pain of the individual. — Zydenbos 2006: 38

However, each of these *karmas* has further subdivisions and there are

> 5 subgroups of knowledge-obscuring *karma*, 9 subgroups of intuition-obscuring *karma*, 2 subgroups of *vedanīya karma*, 28 subgroups of *mohanīya karma*, 4 subgroups of *āyu karma*, 103 subgroups of *nāma karma*, 2 of *gotra karma* and 5 subgroups of *antarāya karma*. — Tater 2009: Contents

One may not think of any further subdivisions of *karma*. Each subgroup takes one to a newer understanding of how minutely the laws of the cosmos work.

The great philosophy indicates that kārmic particles are material in nature and their substance is *pudgala* (matter), which enacts in aggregates of atoms. The *karma* theory explains

> how *pudgala* particles combine to form larger units; these theories have been compared to Indian as well as non-Indian atomic theories. — Zydenbos 2006: 39

Karma is the law of the universe that acts in a purely rational and scientific way. The Jaina *karma* theory can also be helpful to understand the symmetry in the cosmos.

When one dives a little deeper into the understanding of *karma* as described in Jainism, one feels the immense freedom it provides. For there is no one whom one is answerable to, for any of one's deeds, but to oneself. This understanding equips one to take absolute command of one's life. Interestingly, the *karma* principle is neither something that a God-like authority has applied nor is merely the subject matter to be grasped through emotions. However, it motivates us to keep our eyes open to understand these natural laws and keep strengthening our knowledge about the same through self-study and self-experience to understand the same better. Hence, we see that despite being ancient, "it is based on principles which can be openly and rationally discussed" (Zydenbos 2006: 44). However, the theory, even most of the Jainas emphasize today, is of strict following of ethics. No one pays heed to the fact that even in the very roots of ethics lies the theory of *karma.*

Understanding *karma* philosophy starts from one's own experiences. If one is eating infected food, one is bound to have stomach infection. If one is typing the wrong spellings of a particular word into the computer, the printout will only display the same. Similarly, when one thinks about life beyond death or before birth, one can have this realization that one's present circumstances are the results of the actions performed by one in the past; be it this or any of the prior lives. And the present reactions will act as the cause of the future effects, eventually influencing this life and the lifetimes to come.

> Just as I can harm my health in this life by certain unwise actions, I can harm the quality of my next life by certain other actions.
>
> — Ibid.: 56

No matter how strong or mild a specific *karma* is

> each *karma* has a life and after that it separates out from the *karma* body. The shedding of *karma* from the *karma* body is known as *nirjarā.* — Tater 2009: 29

One of the numerous examples of *nirjarā* in our daily lives is one's efforts towards losing weight. *Nirjarā* (shedding of *karma*) can be done in two ways: one, to let the *karma* finish its lifespan and get separated and the second is through efforts. Whereas we are supposed to exercise and eat a balanced diet to lose the *karma* of excess body weight, we can shed other types of *karma* by performing specific related tasks.

In the *Pañcāstikāya*,[12] referring to the immemorial linkage between the soul and the kārmic matter, it is mentioned:

> The *jīva* (soul) and *karma pudgala* (kārmic matter) are mutually tied deeply. At their time of fruition, the *karma* gives fruits to the soul, in the form of joy and sadness. The *jīva* is bound to endure that fruit. After giving fruit, the *karma* sheds off. —Jalaj 2016: 45

The soul has been caught in this cycle of cause and effect since time immemorial, and this cycle may go on till infinity if the soul remains unawakened. However, it has been mentioned in the ancient texts of wisdom that the moment it awakens through the right knowledge and starts perceiving everything rightly, this cycle becomes finite.

We must peep into the *karma* theory to understand human behavioural patterns and many other complicated emotional and mental issues. Indeed, most of one's traits in the present life are genetic; but the presence of past kārmic accounts is another important instrumental cause.

> The pattern of human actions is set originally during embryonic development under the control of DNA which in itself is partly inherited and partly kārmic. — Tater 2009: 35

Under the microscope of *karma*, even inheritance is kārmic.

By its temperature, the candle draws the wax through the wick and simultaneously converts it into its body (viz. glow); this is what the consciousness does exactly. With its attributes of attachment (*rāga*) and aversion (*dveṣa*), it gathers the material aggregates, which turn into *karma* through its activities. For example, a desire to construct a new house motivates one to earn money, buy land, prepare maps, take the required grants from the respective departments, hire an architect, labourers, etc., and even after the house is made, one has to maintain it to keep it clean and up-to-

---

12 *jīvāḥ pudgalakāyāḥ anyonyāvagāḍhagrahaṇapratibaddhāḥ* ।
kāle viyujyamānāḥ sukhaduḥkhaṁ dadita bhuñjanti ॥
— *Pancãstikāya* 2.67

date continuously. This is the simple example of binding *karmas* through the soul's efforts of attachment.

When discussing the solitariness of the infinite journey of life and death, one contemplates why others come in touch with one, in the form of different relationships, etc., and how others' *karmas* are associated with one. To solve this query, the following statement can be helpful:

> You don't live with consequences of other people's *karma*. You live with the consequences of your own. — Tripathi 2010: 144

And these consequences are not only caused but also their effect is endured by oneself and no other. However, different relationships, events and personalities come into the picture to bring these consequences in front of us.

In Indian culture, glimpses of a deeper understanding of *karma* theory can be traced almost in every household, from the words of the elders. For example, thinking of different, complicated relationships as the reason for settling some previous kārmic account. In the context of clearing of kārmic accounts, Brian Weiss (2000: 55) writes: "you progress by paying your debts. You determine what must be done to pay that debt". Here lies the freedom of that specific individual, as one is supposed to choose how the accounts would be cleared. Be it the context of relationships or any other, each of us has to endure many ups and downs that bother us. But if we start to see and analyse everything under the canopy of kārmic accounts, the image begins to get clearer, and we start having faith in not carrying over the account further but in clearing it here and now. This is the beauty of *karma* philosophy that it leaves no stone unturned, even in improvising a person.

Often one doubts why one has to endure the most from one's closest relationships. The alphabets, especially in Hindi that are spoken using the same parts of our speech mechanism belonging to the same family, are being written and also kept together in the chart. An alphabet from the other group has nothing much to do with a specific group of alphabets until used in a word. We can see relationships in the same light.

> Relationships are a living laboratory, a field test to determine how we are doing, whether our lessons have been learned.
>
> — Weiss 2000: 60

They are relationships that keep taking one's tests to check if one has truly evolved during the journey of life or not.

Often, we are taught to focus on materialistic success; surprisingly, no one tells us what we will take when we depart from this world. One has to conclude the same on one's own, through his life's experiences and observations that

> when we die and our souls progress to higher dimensions, we take our behaviours, our deeds, our thoughts and our knowledge with us. — Ibid.: 64

And not even a bit of materialistic possessions travel with us in our future journeys. This contemplation motivates one to peep within and enhances the ethics in each dealing of one's life. One transforms when one realizes "one will not meet one's possessions in the afterlife, but one's loved ones" (ibid.), whom one loses during the journey of life and whose separation seemed unbearable.

> *Karma* in Jainism is a form of subtle matter that encases the soul. By doing so it obscures knowledge and understanding of reality. — Mardia and Rankin 2013: 34

The beauty of the Jaina *karma* philosophy lies in its scientificness; when one realizes that there is no one to keep account of one's *karma*, one becomes confident and takes command of one's life in his own hands. This is but the need of the hour. When everyone has lost self-confidence and looking up to some divine power for help, Jaina philosophy teaches one to be independent through its well-elaborated *karma* doctrine.

The subatomic matter, of which kārmic matter is made, is called *karmons*. These tiny *karmons* roam around in space without interacting with each other, but at the same time, they have the attribute of getting united with similar particles as and when needed.

> *Karmons* are unique in the sense that they can only be absorbed by the soul, and cannot fuse by themselves.
>
> — Mardia and Rankin 2013: 68

Hence, individually they do not harm the consciousness; they can only enact when they are in conjunction with the soul. Each action of the consciousness attracts *karmons* towards it, *karmons* that come and stick with it according to the intensity of the intent of the soul, which eventually decides the duration of their stay. The more the aggregates of *karmons*, the heavier one's kārmic baggage is.

When an evil person comes in contact with a good human being, gradually, the goodness influences; though the good one has his own journey that has nothing to do with the bad one, the good one still influences the bad one in some way or the other. Though the good person will not stay with the bad one forever, he still leaves a mark on the bad person's character, which may eventually bring positive changes in his persona. Also, there is an equal possibility that if the bad person is stronger and more intense in his ways than the good one, the effect can be reversed. This way, despite having their own individual journeys, both of them affect each other.

Similarly, the soul being the non-material substance, none of the kārmic matters gets really attached to the soul. However, it gets influenced by the surrounding *karmons*, which alter its character. The effect of the positive or negative kārmic matter, along with the perverted or righteous energy field of the consciousness, creates a force field, which causes the influx of the kārmic matter towards the soul. "Both these effects are part of an aspect of reality known to the Jainas as *āsrava*" (ibid.: 71). *Āsrava* occurs from all directions at all times, as the consciousness is never bereft of action. Now the kārmic force field couples with the energy field of the soul and encases it accordingly.

We call this process kārmic fusion, but in traditional Jaina terms, it is an aspect of *bandha.*

In simpler language, *āsrava* is the door through which newer *karma* continuously enters the soul's ambit and fuses with the previously present *karmas* and the soul's energy field. The intensity of intent at the time of performing that specific *karma* plays a vital role in this process, as it decides the other factors of the newly-bound *karmas*, i.e. type, duration, etc.

Leśyā or Kārmic Colourations

The mental and emotional garbage we carry inside surrounds us all the time and conveys the same energy to others; this is why we feel positive after meeting someone and drained after meeting the other. Today, people may call it aura or vibes, but the Jaina philosophy has a more profound word for that, which is *leśyā* (thought colours). *Leśyā* has been defined as:

> The temper of the soul in its union with *kaṣāya* (i.e. anger, pride, deceit and greed) that reflects through its mind, speech and bodily actions.
> — Varni 2014b: 420

Another definition has been given as "that which besmears the soul with *karmas* (ibid.). To simplify even further, *leśyā* can be defined as "the kārmic stain of the soul" (Flügel 2014: 62).

Karma can be performed in three ways, i.e. thoughts, speech and deeds (*mana*, *vacana* and *kāya*); together, they are called *yoga* (activity). As each of the actions cannot be performed without the involvement of emotions such as anger, pride, deceit or greed, with infinitely varying degrees of intensity, from one being to another. Hence, we observe:

> In mundane life, *yoga* is inextricably woven together with passions. One cannot be divorced from the other.
> — Sogani 2001: 53

Leśyā surrounds one at all times. The six types of *leśyā* correspond to the six types of the intensity of passions – from most intense to the mildest – they are called *kṛṣna* (black), *nīla* (blue), *kāpota* (grey), *pīta* (yellow), *padma* (lotus-pink) and *śukla* (luminous white), respectively. The first three are inauspicious and represent heavy kārmic density, while the latter three are auspicious and represent the opposite. Hence, they condition good and bad deeds (*puṇya* and *pāpa*). All six types of kārmic colourations indicate the attitude of the different individuals, from the most violent to the most compassionate. Each emotion matters, each action and its intention inevitably gets recorded into the camera of the universe, and all of us get the printout of the picture at the right time. This is the beauty of *karma*, where *leśyā* plays an important role.

An example of six individuals is given to explain the different colourations of *leśyā*. While the first individual with black *leśyā*, thinks of uprooting the tree to have its fruits, the second one with blue, thinks of cutting the tree from its trunk. The third one, with grey *leśyā*, considers cutting off the branches; the fourth, with yellow, contemplates to break off the parts of the branches; the fifth, with lotus-pink, plucks the ripened fruit; whereas the one with the most auspicious, luminous white *leśyā*, picks up the ripened fruit that has fallen on the ground. This way

> *leśyā* also highlights the importance of preserving the environment and working with the nature rather than seeking to exploit or conquer it. — Mardia and Rankin 2013: 82

Needless to say that *leśyā* is also about all the various degrees between the six colourations; it applies not only to nature but to each of life's occurrences. Hence, the concept of *leśyā* in Jaina philosophy is also the pinnacle of friendliness with the environment and self-introspection.

Shedding of karma (nirjarā)

In spite of liberation appearing to be a far-fetched state, one thing can be observed surely, one feels lighter in a state of positive thoughts and even lighter in a state of equanimity. This is but the gist of *nirjarā*. As each soul's ultimate purpose is to attain *mokṣa*, the soul needs to shed off each of its accumulated *karmas*. We see that the purer the consciousness, the lighter its kārmic baggage, and the more impurity indicates the heavier baggage. *Nirjarā* has been simplified as "falling of the previously bonded *karma*" (Varni 2014a: 621). Each of the beings keeps shedding *karma* and, in turn, keeps binding new *karma* according to its intent while performing that action. Hence, we see that whatever one does, intent matters the most, for only intent decides what type of *karma* one is binding, until when it will be bound and what will be the fruit.

> The time to decay and the corresponding potential strength of each component is fixed by the degree of passions with which the activity takes place. — Mardia and Rankin 2013: 114

Besides the intent at the time of performing a specific *karma*, the inner state of various degrees of each of the four passions, i.e. anger, pride, deceit and greed, also decides all the other factors of *karma*.

> Once the *karmon* had its impact, it is transmitted from the spirit, coming back to an undifferentiated state and in this manner to the limitless pool of free *karmons*. — Ibid.

However, that does not mean that the same *karmon* can never be attracted by the same soul again; it may return, again and again, to the *jīva* according to its passions and intensity.

Amazingly, violence can only be done in mind, speech and physical actions: to oneself and to someone else. Each bears different negative results for the individual. The beauty of *karma* theory is that one cannot perform any action for someone else but is inevitably bound to do *karma* for oneself only. Whenever it appears that one is doing any service to others by ons's actions, it has to be observed that this service binds lighter *karma* for oneself only and not for others. Hence, "helping others towards *mokṣa* with positive non-violence results in the lightest new kārmic matter" (Mardia and Rankin 2013: 118).

Though the path of *mokṣa* is quite a far one, to begin with, if one is knowledgeable and unconditionally shares that knowledge with everyone, one attracts lighter kārmic matter for oneself.

Driving a car requires utmost carefulness as it is a powerful vehicle, which, if not taken care of well while being driven, can cause the demise of anyone's life, even of the one driving. Hence, along with remembering the route, the driver must be skilful and mindful. To understand *karma* and its importance on the path of spiritual upliftment, this analogy can be fitted well, where any carelessness leads to the degradation of one's journey. However, once he develops awareness, he takes control of his life and gets it back on track.

Knowingly or unknowingly, we continuously strive for bigger, better and more beautiful through each endeavour. But most of the time, this attempt is materialistic. Rarely do we get to know that, eventually, each of us is searching for our true nature, which is blissful and peaceful. One on a spiritual path is bound to contemplate *karmas* and their shedding. A seeker knows "as the *karmons* are shed, there will be an increase in the energy, allowing further spiritual growth" (Mardia and Rankin 2013: 132). It is like one step leads to another and so on. Shedding of *karma* particles helps the being realize its true nature, eventually enhancing its energy.

Human life, the most developed manifestation of consciousness, can either manipulate and annihilate or contribute to flourishing any life form on the planet. However, it is a matter of concern that we are focusing our energy on the prior. Despite being dependent on various life forms in various ways, we are carelessly and thoughtlessly wiping them out forever, at a rate of many species a day. In this context:

> Jaina insights into *karma*, that prompt and coddle every wild and refined soul, are remarkably timely. — Tobias 1991: 75

It is wonderful that the real religion, or call of duty, starts from within; when one has innumerable questions, one introspects into the self and finds answers to most of them. The Jaina *karma* theory is like digging deeper into the self to find the purest of treasures within. Treasures of the consciousness which do not harm nature but work with it.

Karma in the light of cause and effect

Karma is a complicated network of series of cause and effect, where each *karma* takes us back a distance in time. Each present *karma* is the effect of some previous *karma* that worked as a cause for the same, and at the same time, that previous *karma* was the effect of some other previous *karma* that must have caused it and one's present reaction to specific *karma* enacts as the cause of the future *karma* and so on. In current times when religions have been described as irrational and fearful and the way they are becoming chaotic, the Jaina *karma* theory makes us feel free and independent.

The whole purpose of studying the *karma* philosophy is to apply this wisdom in our daily lives, where we can see the bigger picture under the vision of cause that has been created by us back in time; and, in effect, the situation we are facing at present. When one gets hold of the *karma* theory, one understands deeply that one's present circumstances have been laid down by oneself in the past, and when one gets aware of it, one questions one's agony, which seems pointless. Famous scholar Robert Zydenbos has said:

> The core of Jainism is (a) the *karma* doctrine, (b) the metaphysical dualistic polarity, recognizing *jīva* and *ajīva*, (c) its very typical epistemology and ontology (which is the true basis of Anekāntavāda and Syādvāda). Everything else is derived from this, including the Jaina system of ethics. This is very important to realize: ethics is not the starting point, but a consequence of other thoughts. The Jainas themselves have forgotten this and want to believe that their religion is non-violence and nothing else. If anyone who has been philosophically trained critically

> thinks about this for more than one minute, it will be clear why this cannot be true.[13]

Hence, under the canopy of *karma*, we can improvise and lead a more peaceful and happier life. Especially the detailed description of *karma* in Jaina philosophy is so logical that it leaves no query unanswered; rather, it inspires its students for self-introspection and makes them understand that if anyone can be reformed in the world, it is "me". If each individual in our society would start working on self-improvement through self-introspection, healthy self-criticism and self-analysation, that day is not far when peace will prevail on our planet.

Theory of Knowledge

Gaining knowledge about all circumstances is immensely beautiful. When veils of ignorance lift from the consciousness, what appears is the vibrant sun of enlightenment that displays the path ahead that, despite having occasional rough patches, portrays streams of bliss and is the only way to reach out to the true nature of the self.

In Jaina philosophy, knowledge plays the most crucial role in the upliftment of the soul. There is no escape from it because without the quest to know one can never have a clearer perception of things or events. In fact, knowledge, along with perception, is the characteristic possessed by consciousness and to attain enlightenment, one requires the trio of right knowledge, right perception and right conduct. Ācārya Umāsvāti mentions:[14]

> The enlightened world view, enlightened knowledge and enlightened conduct are the paths to liberation. —Tatia 2011: 5

The right world view motivates one to seek and gain the right knowledge and together they show the path towards the right conduct. An important aspect of Jainism, which is often ignored

---

[13] As told in an e-mail interview on 30 August 2016.

[14] *samyag-darśana-jñāna-cāritrāṇi mokṣamārgaḥ* । — *Tattvārthasūtra* 1.1

even by the Jainas is that merely following the ethics without in-depth knowledge is an incomplete process.

The most important perspective of any religious philosophy is that it introduces one to one's true nature, which is freedom.

> The world view which sees many and the whole is enlightened.
> It avoids dogmas which inhibit free and open thought. — Ibid.

Each seeker of truth travels from the relative viewpoint to the absolute one, which inculcates the shallow to deep layers of relativity. Hence, the more one is spiritually enlightened, the calmer and more understanding one becomes.

Beautifully, the journey of gaining clearer perception and knowledge runs parallelly. A better perception to see and understand things, situations, objects and people enacts as the reason, which motivates one to know more about the same. Knowledge gaining is a chain reaction, where each gained knowledge gives way to the higher planes of knowledge, eventually leading to spiritual upliftment.

> Enlightened world view is the cause, enlightened knowledge and conduct the effect. — Tatia 2011: 5

No matter what, a seeker moves ahead on the path of knowledge only when she/he feels an intuition, a perception or a quest to know more. Hence, the enlightened world view is placed before enlightened knowledge and, together, they lead the seeker to adopt enlightened conduct that works in absolute harmony with nature and determines the spiritual path.

The eminent scholar of Jaina philosophy, Nathmal Tatia, editor and translator of the *Tattvārthasūtra*, negates the single path doctrines:

> The doctrines of knowledge alone, faith alone or conduct alone can never be considered as the right path to liberation.
>
> — Ibid

Not only that, but the emphasis on the rightness of knowledge, perception and conduct has been given equal importance in the philosophy of Jainism. For example, to know how to manufacture a weapon of destruction and to know how to save lives from that both fall into the categories of knowledge, but needless to indicate which one is right.

The existence of the opposites is well established.

> Whatever appears as the unshakeable truth, the exact opposite may also be true in another context. — Tripathi 2010: 324

For example, the strength, the kind of bone structure a *tīrthaṁkara* possesses, has a purpose of absolute self-realization; on the contrary, a denizen of the seventh hell also possesses the same bone structure and strength, needless to mention that it is far away from self-realization. Hence, in Jaina philosophy, there is much emphasis on gaining the right knowledge, for it is the most essential ingredient that helps one attain Godhood.

> Our task is to learn, to become God-like through knowledge. We know so little ... by knowledge we approach God. — Weiss 2000: 1

And through knowledge, we not only find ways for ourselves but also become able to guide others. Only knowledge can introduce us to the soul-God to whom this journey belongs.

Also, irrespective of how intelligent one is, one cannot start the journey towards knowledge or spiritual discipline on one's own. One must seek guidance from those ahead on the same path, be it a *guru* (a teacher) or a philosopher.

> We pass on knowledge to each other, so every generation begins its journey from the shoulders of the previous generation and not from the scratch. — Tripathi 2011: 48

Every generation of truth seekers redefines knowledge a little further, according to their time and understanding of the laymen; hence, even the *tīrthaṁkaras* are called the reformers and not the founders of the natural laws.

> One of the most important of life's lessons is to learn independence, to understand freedom. — Weiss 2000: 69

We gain empirical or indirect knowledge through our senses and mind; whereas senses observe the surroundings, the mind puts the same through the sieve of rationality. However, direct knowledge does not fall into the ambit of senses and mind. Ācārya Umāsvāti mentions:[15]

> The enlightened world view may arise spontaneously or through learning. — Tatia 2011: 6

In our daily lives, we may find a few examples of the same. We observe an average child who has a keen interest in gaining knowledge; we see him as a genius after a few years. An example of an enlightened world view that emerges spontaneously can be — we meet a woman who talks quite normally about her husband, children, shopping and how much she loves being a homemaker. But when we meet the same woman after a few months, we get mesmerized by her transformation; now, she talks about success, motivation, career and life's bigger purpose. According to the ancient philosophy, the beginningless journey of consciousness cannot be traced with logic.

> The soul transmigrates from one birth to the next according to its *karma*, which determines its destiny. — Ibid.

Here, the beautiful thing to note is that each consciousness, despite being individual, shares the same attributes as all the other individual souls, be it in the body of a dog, a mosquito or a human. Hence,

> each unique soul possesses the inherent knowledge and intuition which can empower it to destroy the beginningless deluded world view tormenting it. — Ibid.

Even beings like lions, dogs, cats and cows can attain an enlightened world view and progress onto the spiritual path, for

---

15 *tan nisargād adhigamādvā* । — *Tattvārthasūtra* 1.3

it is the soul's journey and not the body's in which it manifests according to its *karma*.

The secrets of the universe, the origin of planets, the beginning of time, these subjects belong to the truth. The truth, which is not dependent on any factor, rather exists. Any person who experiences the nature of reality does not discover it but feels it and describes it with in the ambit of available vocabulary. Even

> Bhagavān Mahāvīra was not the founder of the truth but one who expressed it in the limitations of language. — Acarya 2003: 145

This is the irony of any language that not only the truth but also a specific feeling or even an emotion can only be expressed unto a limit; beyond that, it can only be experienced.

Irrespective of our arguments of having faith in rationality, we may admit that even rationality has its limitations, and even a rational person enacts under intuition.

> Thinking and reasoning belong to a lower plane; intuition (*darśana*) begins where reasoning ends. — Mahaprajna 2013: 4

For example, a passionate dreamer may intuitively see his distant, successful future, whereas he has to work rationally to reach that state. However, he cannot describe logically that he already knew that he would achieve this success one day. Hence, we see that perception enacts at a superior stratum beyond the conditioning of mind and regular thoughts.

Types of Knowledge

In the philosophical text *Tattvārthasūtra*,[16] there are five types of knowledge:

> Empirical, articulate, clairvoyant, mind-reading and omniscient knowledge. — Tatia 2011: 12

Each type of knowledge is a ladder to move onto the path of higher dimensions of knowledge and spiritual discipline.

---

16 *mati-śrutā-vadhi-manaḥparyāya-kevalānī jñānaṁ* । — 1.9

> Empirical knowledge (cognition) is gained through the senses and/or the mind's ability to comprehend what is sensed. — Ibid.

Mati-jñāna (empirical knowledge) is the first and the most basic way to gain knowledge for each living being, from the moment we arrive in this world till we leave.

> Articulate knowledge refers to conceptualization through language. — Tatia 2014: 12

The knowledge we gain through the senses and the mind requires words for expression; hence, this knowledge is called *śruta-jñāna*. Though words have their limitations, they display an enhanced vision of a particular object, which helps one make others understand the same, along with clearing the concept in one's intellect.

> Clairvoyance refers to the perception of things that are out of the natural range of the senses. — Ibid.

Though even self-realization occurs beyond senses and the mind, clairvoyance (*avadhi-jñāna*) is the knowledge of the history of one's journey of many lifetimes. Tatia mentions:

> In humans, clairvoyance is acquired through spiritual discipline, whereas, for the inhabitants of heaven and hell, it is inborn.
> — Ibid.

To be equipped with the knowledge of the history of one's own journey provides an opportunity not to commit the same mistakes again, due to which a specific being is in a downward vertical dimension (or hell according to the language of the ancient texts) and also to know the reasons of the good things done by that specific being, due to which it is in the upward vertical dimension or heaven. This way, the universe provides ample opportunities for each being to either carry on doing the same type of *karma* in other dimensions or take hold of one's journey through knowledge and fix it.

Being humans, we are at the horizontal dimension where clairvoyance can only be earned through gaining knowledge and practising spiritual discipline; hence, laypeople stay unaware of their roots. But this lack is not to be taken negatively because due to this lack of knowledge, only humans get ample chances to settle their kārmic accounts through their *puruṣārtha* (hard work). We are completely unaware of the reasons for our adverse or favourable circumstances. Being human, being on earth is like a test, the result of which gets decided by our reaction to each happening.

> Mind reading is the act of seeing the objects (the modes) of another's mind. — Tatia 2011: 12

Gaining knowledge gradually takes one to the planes from gross to subtle. While clairvoyance is *avadhi-jñāna*, in which the events in time are remembered, mind reading (*manaḥparyāya-jñāna*) is a step ahead and makes the seeker capable of reading and understanding others' minds. Together with clairvoyance, mind-reading knowledge can do wonders; it also equips the practitioner to travel back in time to see what someone was thinking during a specific occurrence.

> Omniscience refers to knowledge of all substances in all their modes: past, present and future. — Ibid.

This is the ultimate knowledge a spiritualist aims for. A blissful state of knowledge where one is adept at seeing each atom, each being, each object of the entire universe at once, with all its modes in the past, present and future. At this stage, the seeker is called the knower of everything, God. This is a state that every soul can achieve. Hence, we know that only knowledge can take one towards Godhood.

Honourable Ācārya Umāsvāti mentions in the philosophical text *Tattvārthasūtra* 1.10 (*tatpramāṇe*):

> These five varieties of knowledge divide into the two classes of approved means of knowledge, the mediate (acquired) and the immediate (innate). — Tatia 2011: 13

Any knowledge can be acquired in two ways: through the medium of senses and mind, and the immediate knowledge that does not require any medium but is directly perceived by the soul. Whereas the prior comes in the category of indirect knowledge (*apratyakṣa-jñāna*), the latter is the subject matter of direct knowledge (*pratyakṣa-jñāna*).

The next *sūtra* 1.11 depicts *ādye parokṣam*:

> The first two varieties of knowledge, empirical and articulate, are acquired knowledge. — Tatia 2011: 13

As they involve mind and senses, another *sūtra* 1.12 (*pratyakṣaṁ anyat*) mentions:

> The remaining three varieties of knowledge are instances of innate knowledge. — Ibid.

Each individual soul is inevitably equipped with all three types of direct knowledge because, according to the Jaina thinkers, to know and perceive are consciousness's inevitable and inseparable attributes.

A basic query to know falls under the quest of the soul. The mind and senses are the instruments that are operated by the consciousness. The immediate (direct) knowledge is covered by the layers of kārmic matter, which vary highly from one being to another. But, once knowledge gaining starts with an innate desire to know the self, the layers start to shed, and the journey of amazement towards higher spiritual dimensions begins.

> Only omniscience alone arises out of total elimination of knowledge-covering *karma* and therefore knows everything — past, present and future. — Ibid.

Attaining omniscience is the pinnacle of gaining knowledge, for it covers the entire universe in all its modes in all three dimensions of time. Hence, in a strict sense, only omniscience can be called as the direct knowledge.

Knowledge and The Supreme Being

If we are absolutely acquainted with a particular prayer before reciting it and when the prayer is not a eulogy of a an extraordinary personality but our humble reverence to those humans whom we can become like, the prayer holds a different meaning altogether. When there is no discrimination between God and us, the only difference is that we are yet to achieve that state through gaining knowledge.

Considering the beauty of the *ṇamokāra mantra*, we realize that it reminds us of the best possible manifestation of the human form. A state of the highest knowledge and perception, which is accessible not only to humans but also to each being, to win over inner rivals, to break the shackles of the soul's intricate relationship with *karma*, which has been there since time immemorial. The *mantra* is a profound homage to all those who have either conquered their inner adversaries and have attained the best human possibility or are on the way to attain the same. The aim of visiting the temple for the Jainas is not about begging for something from an all-efficient being but a humble reverence for the predecessors to be able to walk on the path towards liberation. This way we see that

> Jainism is a philosophy as well as a spiritual system that transcends ordinary human concerns.
>
> — Mardia and Rankin 2013: 23

Jaina philosophy conveys the essence of universal laws and equality. It does not propagate blind following of a Supreme Being or accepting the inherited beliefs; one is free to explore the truth on one's own, at one's own pace. One is absolutely free to raise questions and find answers using one's rationale. A patient quest to know the reality and, through that, to know the self. No religion-based prejudice, caste does not matter; what is required is the right perception and knowledge which motivate one to adopt the right conduct.

Attaining Right Knowledge

Just as right and wrong knowledge exists,

> right (and wrong) answers do exist but the former cannot be imposed from without. — Mardia and Rankin 2013: 36

There can be a scenario where it becomes difficult to analyse a specific moment's reality. The task one is performing, thinking one is doing a great job, can be a task which is fatal to the lives of other beings. In that particular moment, the right answer, sooner or later, will have to come from within and in most cases, it comes. For example, in the case of Claude Eatherly, "the pilot of the Straight Flush, that supported the dropping of the atomic bomb on Hiroshima, during the Second World War"[17] was somehow unaware of the deadly consequences of his action.

However, when he realized that it caused serious repercussions for millions of people, guilt consumed him and he led a painful life of depression and anxiety afterwards, and even attempted suicide. Ironically, he was declared a "war hero" in America. As repentance, he even "sent parts of his pay check to Hiroshima, writing letters of apology".[18] In his case, the right answer came from within, but after performing that specific action. Ironically, other pilots, too, carried the same duties but never realized the consequences. Hence, we analyse that the knowledge is also supposed to be right. Rightness is not about taking lives but about living in complete harmony with nature.

Also, an intelligent seeker apprehends that "the more he knows, the more he has to learn" (Mardia and Rankin 2013: 36), the very purpose of gaining knowledge is to keep digging, questioning and finding. In this world of many philosophies, through discussions and listening to other perspectives, we find plenty of ideas to be

---

17 "Claude Eatherly", 22 March 2021: <https://en.wikipedia.org/wiki/Claude_Eatherly>.

18 Ibid.

thought upon and question our own beliefs repetitively until we find the most satisfactory answers by polishing our intellect and attaining the pinnacle of the right knowledge.

At a higher plane of our knowledge-gaining journey, we realize that

> all living systems are interconnected and we should see ideas also as parts of a whole, rather than disconnected, abstract concepts. — Mardia and Rankin 2013: 37

As thoughts and ideas also ooze out from consciousness, somewhere, each thought and idea helps one move ahead towards the understanding of the whole truth. This consideration takes one to a platform where one starts respecting each point of view and takes it as an opportunity to grow.

Like science, philosophy also allows one to keep exploring and question one's findings. Humans started to be curious about the secrets of the cosmos with their evolution, but that does not mean that even the universe began to exist since then. Scientists too admit that we know

> just 4 per cent of the universe. The other 96 per cent is made of stuff astronomers can't see, detect or even comprehend.
> — Moskowitz 2011

There is a 100 per cent probability that there are beings that are ahead of us. According to the Jaina philosophical texts, there is "the existence of spiritually advanced life in other parts of the universe" (Mardia and Rankin 2013: 94). Just like we are keeping track of the solar systems and galaxies, there is a possibility that some other kinds of beings are keeping track of our activities. Their consciousness is much ahead of us, spiritually as well as scientifically.

> Indeed the Jaina sensibility views physics and chemistry, astronomy and cosmology, as some of the most important spiritual disciplines. — Ibid.: 127

Not only that, on one's journey towards knowledge, one realizes that these subjects are interlinked. The study of one inevitably takes the seeker to another and so on. This is the fun part, a pinnacle, an amalgamation, when there seems to be no difference between science and spirituality; instead, they become intertwined. To understand one, the other is required to be studied with equal dedication.

Accessing Knowledge

To arrive into this world through parents, to breathe, to grow, to observe and die — all these activities are inevitable and universal, which every living being goes through. Similarly, gaining knowledge and awakening are not meant to be accessed by the special ones belonging to a specific caste, creed, nation or gender. The right knowledge is always about knowing the laws of the universe, which are freely available to be known by all. Hence, "it is possible to be aware of the truth of the teachings of the *tīrthaṁkaras* without even being consciously aware of them" (Mardia and dankin 2013: 148). As the teachings of the *tīrthaṁkaras* belong to the universal truth, they are not biased or discriminating.

The world of knowledge motivates one to question each of one's previous beliefs; for example, "coincidence" is used frequently in our daily vocabulary. However, when one dives deeper into philosophy and the subject of knowledge, one realizes that there is nothing like a coincidence.

> There are reasons for everything and no coincidences exist on the path of destiny. — Weiss 2010: 45

Only the effect caused by one in the past, like finding an efficient teacher or meeting someone even for a minute, is not a coincidence but destiny designed by oneself only.

When one goes through awakening, one ponders — if this is the real me, who was that which was there previously? For this me is something beyond, someone higher than myself. As Michael Tobias shares his experience,

> a quiet revelation purring at the rear of that dark canyon I know to be myself, conveying what I must have known to be true all along.
>
> — 1991: Preface

This is the power of knowledge, accessible to all at all times. To know that reality, which observes and experiences everything. Which is the one writing this and the one reading. That exists, irrespective of anything, for it is the only "conscious" substance that constitutes the cosmos.

Yoga

> *There are many roads to reach a destination; some are more efficient but tough, while some are easier and take long routes.*

There are innumerable paths to finding the truth and *yoga* takes each path towards freedom, where each *yogī* is free to find his path according to his ability. *Yoga* is the collective outcome of the mind, speech and physical activities. Hence, it includes one's whole life. However, in today's world, it is only seen as *āsanas* that help one in maintaining physical and mental discipline.

The recent definition of *yoga* is "a group of physical, mental and spiritual practices or disciplines".[19] Besides the activities related to the mind, body and speech, *yoga* in Jaina philosophy has been described more deeply. "Vibrations of the soul *pradeśa* associated with physical, mental and vocal activities" (Aggarwal 2014: 151) is *yoga*. Here, *pradeśa* refer to the space points occupied by the soul. Just like knowledge and world view are a being's innate attributes, knowingly or unknowingly, the soul keeps exploring these qualities through *yoga*. According to the definition of *yoga*, a being is inevitably performing *yoga* at all times. Hence, in Indian culture, one is advised to be mindful of everything one does, to live each moment consciously.

To align the activities of the mind, speech and physical actions, one needs to be in absolute alignment with the nature that calls for

---

19 "Yoga", < en.wikipedia.org/wiki/Yoga> (accessed on 26 March 2021).

the utmost non-violent way of living. This, in turn, results in five minor vows for the laypeople, known as *aṇuvratas* in Jaina tradition, that the ancient thinkers have decided very thoughtfully. "The *aṇuvratas* are *ahiṁsā, satya, asteya, brahmacarya* and *aparigraha*" which translate into non-violence, truth, non-stealing, celibacy and non-possession respectively.

If one ponders over the concept of non-violence thoughtfully, the realization will dawn upon one that it transcends the boundaries of religion. Non-violence is the simplest universal law. Not only the saints, philosophers, scientists and even mathematicians have had this realization about non-violence but also many great leaders of the world have conceded to its importance. The first query that arises into a seeker's mind is, "As there are innumerable microscopic beings that are harmed in each of one's actions inevitably, how can one stay non-violent?" Ācārya Umāsvāti comforts the seekers of the truth by writing,[20] "taking life away out of passion is violence" (Tatia 2011: 173). In the philosophical text based on the nature of reality, Ācārya Umāsvāti writes about truth[21] and non-stealing,[22] "to speak what is not true is falsehood" (ibid.: 174) and "taking anything that is not given is stealing" (ibid.).

Brahmacarya (celibacy) is much more than abstinence from sexual activities. A *brahmacārī* not only refrains from sexual activities in mind, speech and actions but also stays in a state of realization of the pure soul of oneself and of others. Scholar Jinendra Varni defines *brahmacarya* as

> the *jīva* (soul) is *Brahman*. The meaning of the word *Brahman* is unclouded, knowledgeable soul, and the one who stays absorbed in that state is a *brahmacārī*. — Varni 2014b: 189

Ācārya Umāsvāti further elaborates about the fifth minor vow, i.e.

---

20 *pramattayogāta prāṇavyāpāropaṇama hiṁsā* । — *Tattvārthasūtra* 7.8

21 *asadabhidhānam anṛtaṁ* । — Ibid 7.9

22 *adattānaṁ steyam* । — Ibid 7.10

non-possession,[23] "clinging is possessiveness" (Tatia 2011: 174). At some point in our lives, each of us ponders over the impermanent nature of material possessions, where taking refuge in one's spirit helps one to be at peace. Interestingly, beyond material possessions, Jaina thinkers consider all of one's relationships and emotions as one's possessions, too. The feeling of mineness and belonging to any of these come under delusion. Hence, a seeker is advised to see his kinship and emotions as his possessions.

According to the Jaina tradition, every minute, every action, every thought and eventually one's entire life is the result of *yoga*. Hence, one needs to be cautious in each of one's doing, be it walking, choosing the food and preparing the same for consumption. A *yogī* refrains from harming any creature and tends to live in perfect harmony with nature. It is suggested to align all three, i.e. mind, speech and action.

> There are three forms of self-control (*gupti*): (i) curbing of activity of mind (*mano-gupti*); (ii) curbing of activity of speech (*vāg-gupti*); (iii) curbing of activity of body (*kāya-gupti*). — Williams 1998: 32

We notice that the *yama* in Patañjali's *Yogasūtra* and the *aṇuvrata* for a Jaina layman are exactly the same.

Bāraha Bhāvanās

Moving ahead onto the path of self-purification leads the seeker to twelve *bhāvanās* or the twelve *anuprekṣās*, on which one must contemplate. They are:

> (i) impermanence (*anitya*), (ii) helplessness (*aśaraṇa*), (iii) the cycle of transmigration (*saṁsāra*), (iv) solitariness (*ekatva*), (v) the separateness of the self and the body (*anyatva*), (vi) the foulness of the body (*aśaucya*), (vii) the influx of *karma* (*āsrava*), (viii) the checking of *karma* (*saṁvara*), (ix) the elimination of *karma* (*nirjarā*); (x) the universe (*loka*), (xi) the rarity of

---

[23] *mūrchā parigrahaḥ* । — *Tattvārthasūtra* 7.12

> enlightenment (*bodhi-durlabha*), and (xii) the preaching of the sacred law (*dharma-svākhyāta va*). — Williams 1998: 244

This is what life is about; one lives it, learns from it, ponders over it and yet one is not supposed to indulge in it. Sometimes, with age and, at another, with the happening of a specific incident, favourable or unfavourable, one starts thinking about the bigger purpose of life and one's place in it. These twelve *bhāvanās* are the ones on which one lands safely and then takes off for another journey towards a higher dimension of knowledge and spirituality by analysing the self further.

Yoga and The Awakening of cakras

One of the purposes of Yogic practices is to tap into the source of boundless energy lying idle within; the energy centres *cakras* located in different body parts are practised upon to get them activated. Once activated, these *cakras* can transform one's life. But at the same time, one must prepare oneself to deal with the same energy as it requires a lot of strength. For example:

> The *sahasrāra cakra* (the pineal gland) is the centre of energy. Once activated, it produces strong electric currents.
>
> — Mahaprajna 2013: 16

A mentally and physically weaker body cannot deal with them as these currents, if not taken care of properly, can make one insane. Hence, even for *sādhanā*, one needs a healthy body from within and without.

Those who do *yoga* in the form of postures are aware of the energy it requires. The breathing exercises like *prāṇāyāma*, including *anuloma-viloma*, *kapālabhāti* and *bhastrikā*, may appear simpler. However, they are not. One needs a lot of practice to do them for longer periods. For example, "*Bhastrikāprāṇāyāma* can be performed for a whole hour" (Mahaprajna 2013: 19) and it brings unbelievable beneficial results, physical as well as spiritual.

Yoga and the Final Destination

The final destination in *yoga-sādhanā* is to attain *samādhi*, where the soul is in its purest state, highly knowledgeable and in a state of incessant bliss. Through *yoga*, the practitioner aims to activate the different energy centres in the body so that, in future, they get manifested in higher spiritual and knowledgeable dimensions. "The practitioners season the nervous system to be able to bear still greater strains in higher *sādhanā*" (ibid.) as with heights increase the challenges.

Life is a form of penance; even our dreams fall under the category of *sādhanā*, as they eventually take us towards the bigger purpose. Sudden success, sudden gains, and shortcuts to achieve what one does not deserve can devolve one. One needs to be slow and steady towards one's goal to make the soil fertile to let the seed grow healthily.

> No painter can paint a really beautiful picture unless the canvas on which he paints has been properly prepared.
>
> — Mahaprajna 2013.: 20

Whether becoming prolific writers, painters, entrepreneurs, or sportsmen, we all need a healthy body to pursue our dreams, a favourable familial environment and emotional strength.

In the quest to follow our dreams, we cannot over-exert ourselves. Meditation gives us moments of deep relaxation and spaciousness to rejuvenate, revive and maintain the speed and curiosity towards the destination. Sometimes, it is good to stay away even from what we love to do the most. It only enhances our energy and leaves us with fresher ideas and elated spirits. In attaining higher spiritual dimensions, Jaina Yoga suggests a practice named *kāyotsarga*, "which means complete immobilization of the body" (Ibid.: 35).

When it comes to attaining the final destination or *samādhi* or liberation, Yogic practices like *kāyotsarga* are quite helpful as they lead to the stoppage of kārmic influx and when this closure happens, what happens next is the shedding of previously accumulated *karmas*. As an answer to a question asked by his foremost disciple, Gautama, about *kāyotsarga*, Mahāvīra replied:

> *Kāyaguptī* results in *saṁvara*. *Saṁvara* is a state in which nothing enters into the soul. — Ibid.: 35-36

This way, *kāyotsarga* helps the practitioner feel lighter and as the practice enhances, he is able to access the higher dimensions of bliss.

Hence, contrary to popular belief, "for Jainas, *yoga* means all actions, whether beneficial or harmful, sacred or secular" (Mardia and Rankin 2013: 112). But the purpose is the same, i.e. to attain the best of human possibilities or, in other words, accessing the *Paramātmā* within.

Yoga and Kārmic Bondage

Each action gives way to another action; this is the nature of *karma*. As *yoga* is action, it attracts more *karma*. Whether highly spiritual or miserable, all worldly beings are caught in the kārmic cycle of cause and effect. Though in both examples, the weight of kārlmic bondage varies from lowest to highest degree, even *arhanta* human beings in their supreme state, being empirical souls, are not free of *yoga*. Only

> the *Siddhas* are destitute of all endeavour and hence destitute of *yoga*, for they have no activity of speech, body and mind.
> — Sogani 2001: 48

The state of the *siddha* is the ultimate destination, the ultimate purpose of life's journey, of all the spiritual quests, to know thyself and, through that, to know the universe in its entirety. This is the state each seeker, knowingly or unknowingly, aims for.

Pradeśas are the space points occupied by the soul's actions/*karmas*; each *karma* generates vibrations into the previously present kārmic particles in these space points and, in the process, some *karma* gets shed, and the new ones get bound to the soul. In this way, *āsrava* (inflow of *karma*) and *yoga* are similar. No *yoga* means no action, which eventually means no *āsrava*; hence, the *siddhas* are free from even the tiniest of *āsrava* as they attain the state of no *karma* through their quest to know the knower.

As there are innumerable manifestations of *jīva* in the form of different species, which vary from one-sensed to five-sensed beings, *yoga* is an inevitable trait of each. However, the instruments to perform *yoga* vary from the least developed, as in one-sensed, to the most developed, as in humans. For example, despite being a being, a tree cannot perform *karmas* through its speech and physical actions; it can merely use its subtler faculty that can create cause and endure effects, somewhat similar to the mind.

> Thus, *yoga* prepares the ground for empirical bondage in the presence of other conditions and, consequently, for the perpetuation of worldly career. — Sogani 2001: 48-49

Most of the time, the subtle to gross actions keep the being's view distorted and, through that, keep it bound in the incessant cycle of cause and effect. Or, in rare cases, they motivate one to access the real nature of the self and break the shackles of the same.

Yoga leads to *āsrava*, the inflow of kārmic matter, which in turn gives way to *bandha* (bondage), the sticking process of the kārmic matter around the soul. Intense *yoga* leads to intense *āsrava*, good deeds lead to lighter kārmic matter, and the bad deeds lead to the opposite. Further, it is beautiful to know that only performing *karma* blankly is not enough; one's intention (good, bad or medium) and intensity (sharp, light or mixed) also matter, which decides the period for which that particular *karma* is bound, when ripened, what kind of fruit it will give, how many space points will it cover, etc. Thus, it leads to four classifications of bondage:

> (1) Type bondage (*prakṛti bandha*), (2) space bondage (*pradeśa bandha*), (3) duration bondage (*sthiti bandha*) and lastly, (4) intensity of fruition bondage (*anubhāga bandha*).
>
> — Sogani 2001: 49

There are infinite material particles roaming around freely in space. However, they can be transformed into kārmic particles,

> The vibratory activity of the soul causes them to transform; this has been assigned as type-bondage. — Ibid.

Hence, the *karma* itself decides *prakṛti bandha*. For example, a person steals something out of sheer helplessness under compelling circumstances; otherwise, he is honest and ethical. We observe that the type of *karma* he binds would be lighter in nature. This also depicts the accuracy of the cosmos, as in Jaina philosophy, *karma* is nothing but natural laws.

Space is inevitably occupied by something or the other; in the context of the space points occupied by the soul, it is always kārmic particles. These kārmic particles share a specific relationship with the space points around that specific soul. They get attracted to it "through the same agency of *yoga*" (ibid.) and this process is called space bondage. When the space points of the soul are absolutely free of *karma*, it becomes the Supreme Soul (*Paramātmā*).

If one has sown the seeds of a particular tree, one gets the fruits of the same, according to its time of fruition. Similarly, each seed has its own time of giving fruits, which differs from others. The process of the seed transforming into the tree gets executed under certain laws. Likewise,

> the incessant continuation of the kārmic particles, in association with the self up to a certain period of time, is called duration bondage (*sthiti bandha*). — Sogani 2001: 50

At the time of performing a specific action, each being has some intensity of thoughts, whether mild or strong; this intensity also contributes to deciding the quality of the fruit.

> The effect-producing potency with which the kārmic particles become impregnated is known as intensity of fruition bondage (*anubhāga bandha*). — Ibid.

Now, the intensity of sowing the seed matters, as well as how one takes care of the plant by watering it at appropriate times, the weather conditions, etc. Some trees give fruits only once in their lifetime and some for many consecutive years. Beautifully, examples of the laws of the universe can easily be observed in our surroundings, be it the theory of *karma* or any other.

Yoga and Kaṣāya (Passions)

Life of each being goes on surrounded by *karma* at all times. One can never be without *karma*, which in turn is supported and induced by the four soul-soiling emotions, viz. *krodha* (anger), *māna* (pride), *māyā* (delusion) and *lobha* (greed). Together they keep the soul's journey bound in life, death and rebirth.

> *Sthiti bandha* and *anubhāga bandha* are caused by these four emotions, which are responsible for the defiled state of existence.
>
> — Sogani 2001: 50

At the same time, *karma* can be performed by the soul in a relatively pure state, which is without *kaṣāya*. This results in the destruction of soul-soiling emotions, and the absence of these four emotions leads to the cessation of *yoga*, as a result of which no new *karma* is bound. For example, sometimes, one gets lost in doing the thing one loves the most. So much so that one not only loses track of time but also enters a dimension where one is not expecting anything in return. In these moments, one is beyond these *kaṣāya* and finds shelter in oneself. In the *Bhagavadgītā*,[24] this type of *karma* is known as *niṣkāma karma*, which means selfless or desireless action. This kind of *karma* stops the inflow (*āsrava*) and what happens next is the shedding of the accumulated *karma*.

Often, with age or due to some other circumstances in life, most of us start the journey towards self-introspection, which takes us within, to control unnecessary emotions. We also start

---

24 "Nishkam Karma", yogapedia.com, <https://www.yogapedia.com/definition/6622/nishkam-karma> (accessed on 17 April 2021).

contemplating the real purpose of life and the role of self-improvement. Amongst us, a few people work in the direction to achieve their dreams and, through that, to serve the society. Immersing oneself in a specific dream that fills one with positivity tells one that one is meant to accomplish this in one's life, where there is no expectation but an innate satisfaction of being closer to the self. In these moments, a person attains the state of *niṣkāma karma*. A state of "action without passion, which is a matter of self-achievement" (Sogani 2001: 50). This supports that "*yoga* may exist with or without passions in the life of an individual" (ibid.).

This way, we see that *yoga* connects us to a higher purpose that includes each moment of our lives, the elaborate study of which take us to the detailing of *karma*, how they are bound, how one can stop their inflow, how one can shed them to move ahead towards the pinnacle of the spiritual ladder known as liberation.

Non-Absolutism (Anekāntavāda, Syādvāda and Nayavāda)

The doctrine of Nayavāda expresses the limitations of language to represent experiences and the human inability to understand the complete truth. What one understands through a statement can be entirely different from what the other sees and everybody's understanding can be partially correct. Therefore, we must respect every opinion because every opinion has an element of truth and there is no (one) absolute truth.

Anekāntavāda

The doctrine of Anekāntavāda describes the real nature of all substances (*dravya*) in the universe, which states that every living and non-living entity has infinite modes (*paryāya*) that coexist simultaneously. However,

> they are manifested under different conditions at different times. Thus, the nature is multifaceted and multi-layered.
>
> — Bhandari and Pokharna 2017: 18

The statement, "the truth is one and absolute", is incorrect in the light of Anekāntavāda. The truth is present in many layers in the form of different modes and attributes; one needs to observe and analyse innumerable perspectives to understand the complete truth. Anekāntavāda helps one in approaching the truth through multiple points of views. Just like a woman is a mother at the time of pampering her children, a wife when she is looking after her husband, a businesswoman at the time of carrying on her business responsibilities and a homemaker while looking after her home. We notice that each object innately acquires numerous properties which exist together without meddling with one another. At any given time, only a few qualities get expressed, while others stay dormant and only emerge when the right time comes. This way, it is nearly impossible to know all aspects of its reality at once.

> This theory of multiplicity of nature of an object has been called Anekāntavāda and it has been variously described as multifacetedness, multidimensionality, relativism, non-equivocality, pluralism, contextuality, non-onesidedness, non-absolutism, etc. — Ibid.: 19

Amongst plenty of other examples in our surroundings, one specimen can be analysed – each student carries a genius within along with innumerable other traits, while some can refine that with the help of a good teacher and self-efforts. Others remain unaware and spend their lives in ignorance, finding solace only through exploring the shallow waters of the ocean.

Ācārya Amṛtacandra (tenth century CE) portrayed Anekāntavāda in the following manner:

> Any real object in the world is existent (*sat*) as well as non-existent (*asat*), one and many, eternal (*nitya*) and non-eternal (*anitya*), describable (*abhilāpya*) and indescribable (*anabhilāpya*), neither this nor that, but both, i.e. this as well as that, in terms of its nature, time, space, material and mode (*svabhāva*, *kāla*, *kṣetra*, *dravya* and *bhāva*). — Bhandari and Pokharna 2017: 19-20

For example, a being exists in that specific form through a physical perspective, but from a philosophical point of view, this particular form of that being is merely a temporary manifestation caused by its *karma*. In the case of a human, he is one as a man, but as he performs many duties as a father, employer, husband, driver, son, brother, etc., he is many. He is eternal from the point of view of the journey of consciousness and non-eternal from the viewpoint of this specific appearance. His visible attributes are describable, but as he still has some hidden attributes, they are indescribable as well. He is neither only a husband nor only a son, but both in terms of his nature, according to the time, space and so on.

At all times, we seek a peaceful environment not only at a personal level but also collective. A society where there are no conflicts but a better understanding of others' views and respect for all opinions. If we ask for one theory that can establish peace among humans, that is undoubtedly Anekāntavāda.,

> which leads to the concepts of mutual respect, compromise, tolerance and forgiveness for each other's views and is essential for coexistence and peaceful living. — Ibid.: 20

Anekāntavāda and Syādvāda seem to be there not only to have a better understanding of matter and consciousness but also to show mankind a way to foster mutual understanding amongst families, states, nations and eventually the world.

Mahāvīra was the most prominent philosopher of his time, as he covered all the aspects of reality despite the limitations of language. And to describe that limitation, he introduced Anekāntavāda to his pupils to give them a more profound understanding of the truth.

> Several other concepts, e.g. Syādavāda (contextual perspective), Nayavāda (specific viewpoints), Saptabhaṅgī (seven modes of existence), etc. arose from Anekāntavāda as a result of the teachings of Mahāvīra (599–527 BCE).
>
> — Bhandari and Pokharna 2017: 20

A vow is a pledge one takes from the depths of one's conscience to live life with all honesty and dedication. In the context of the vow of truthfulness, one is supposed to express whatever one says in a manner that depicts respect and, simultaneously, is true. To emphasize this practice, Mahāvīra instructed his pupils not to explain,

> anything without qualifying it with the word *syāt* (in some context), otherwise the statement will become false. — Ibid.

What if all the seekers of the world, instead of imposing themselves on others, stop invalid expectations and start using the word *syāt* that, brother, in some contexts, I am right and in some, you. Hence, let us live peacefully together and work towards making this world a better place.

Any beautiful philosophy or thought remains undiscovered until it becomes known to those who value and understand it. Till then, that thought, that philosophy keeps lying idle. This is precisely what happened to the base of Indian logic, which was there in solitude for over 1,000 years in subjects like Anekāntavāda, Syādavāda and Saptabhaṅgī.

> Till scholars like J.B.S. Haldane (1957) and P.C. Mahalanobis (1954-57) realized their importance in terms of theory of statistics and probability and D.S. Kothari (1985) found its predictions in the context of wave–particle duality akin to the explanations given by quantum theory. — Ibid: 21

In the same decade of the 1980s,

> G.N. Ramachandran (1980, 1982, 1983), in a series of papers, used Syād Nyāya System (SNS) to develop computer logic and worked out a new formulation of Sentenial Logic and its isomorphism with Boolean Algebra. — Bhandari and Pokharna 2017: 21

This way, Anekāntavāda fell into the right hands of scholars and scientists, and it not only helped them discover newer scientific ideas but also made them believe in the Jaina logic prescribed more than 2,500 years back by Mahāvīra.

If someone tells poor, uneducated parents that their child will be a rich, educated and famous man in future, as soon as a child is born, they will feel happy for sure but would not believe such a statement. And if this statement turns out to be true in the long run, the parents will be stunned. This example depicts that every incident, every happening is not observable in all its modes at any specific time, but the different attributes, or modes, become visible as and when the right time comes,

> depending on the context, cause, interaction with environment, time, place, etc. — Ibid.

The best example to support this statement is: someone can become a writer, but this quality remains dormant until she comes in touch with some events or situations around her that help her bring out the writer within. In our daily lives, we can observe examples where a dumb student becomes a genius after coming under the guidance of an efficient teacher or when, in a traumatic event, someone known to be a coward steps ahead and takes charge to take everyone out of it.

Normally, in our daily lives, we tend to react aggressively and instantly whenever a conflict happens in any of our relations. However, with age, we learn to be calm and analyse the possibilities of the reasons for specific strife. Hence, the elderly teach the young to adopt a calm approach, whether dealing with adversity or getting lured by the present moment's attractions, to take any decision spontaneously. A wise decision considers all the aspects and other possibilities to reach a certain conclusion, which may be "presently hidden and indescribable and manifest in future" (Bhandari and Pokharna 2017: 25). Be it choosing a life partner or starting a new business or a job, a well thought-out decision is more durable and beneficial. Therefore, the habit of not reacting instantly results in our peace of mind and we become better and more understanding.

When we meet someone, as part of human nature, we start to develop some judgement about that person. However, we have yet to learn about his past, his way of dealing with situations, his familial background, etc. But we still build some imaginary castles around his persona. Some of our judgements may be right; on the other hand, some may be proven to be the opposite. The more we spend time with that person, the more we learn about his character, choices, strengths, weaknesses, etc. Some take shape with time and circumstances, and some emerge independently as time passes. This indicates:

> There can be multiple ways, views and approaches to comprehend reality. Each view is incomplete in itself but different views complement each other and, together, they give a more wholesome understanding of reality.
>
> — Bhandari and Pokharna 2017: 25

There is also a possibility that even after spending many years with the same person, one day, we suddenly realized that we have not understood him at all. This strengthens that

> the number of modes in which a given "thing" (or a person as in this example) can exist are many, very large or even infinite.
>
> — Ibid.

Then, one fine day, we make peace with the same person. This theory can be applied to each issue around us, not only to understand human behaviour, but also to figure out even more complicated subjects like how the universe works.

One may wonder how Anekāntavāda is needed to understand even Anekāntavāda itself.

> [As] Anekāntavāda has been variously interpreted as the theory of manifoldedness, multifacetedness, multilayered, multisidedness, multiperspective view, contextuality, pluralism, coexistentialism, non-absolutism, non-equivocality and relativism, S. Mookerji (1994) calls it the theory of non-one-sidedness, implying the many-sided nature of reality. — Bhandari and Pokharna 2017: 26

It is the theory of manifoldness as any given attribute of a person or matter may have countable as well as uncountable ways to be seen and analysed; it means each of them is diversified. It is the theory of multifacetedness, as it has many aspects or sides. For example, jewels are often called multifaceted because they have many facets; they are made in such a way that they reflect more and more light to attract a large number of people. Similarly, a being or an object has many facets simultaneously. Anekāntavāda is multilayered as it motivates one to peel off the several layers of truth.

It is the theory of multisidedness as it depicts multiple dimensions; for example, one is a businessman when he is in the middle of a deal, suddenly he gets a call from his daughter, he instantly enters into the dimension of being a father and as soon as he puts the phone down, he comes back into the character of a businessman. It is the theory of multiperspective views as to understand a given situation; one needs to adopt many perspectives as one point of view cannot provide the whole idea of a specific. It is contextual, as in any discussion; we need to analyse the context in which we are talking. It may also be called pluralism as in the quest of understanding the real nature of matter or consciousness; two or more modes, groups of attributes, principles, sources of authority, etc., coexist in them, which eventually gives birth to the theory of coexistentialism.

Syādavāda (The theory of contextual perspective)

One of the fundamental branches of Anekāntavāda is Syādvāda, which depicts the restrictions of language in understanding the truth. It mainly insists that each description is partially right. It depends on which context we are talking about. Hence, whenever there is an argument, discussion or debate, we must understand the context of each of the arguers. Each person understands the same concept through their perspective, which may be not only different and at the same time unique in comparison to others but also right. For example, water satiates one's thirst whenever one is thirsty, despite being in the coolness of an air conditioner. It does the same to someone roaming around in the hot desert, but the degree of thirst varies in both examples. Hence, both are thirsty, but the way each perceives the need to drink water differs significantly.

Syādavāda indicates that each statement, no matter with how much emphasis it is uttered, is partially true and must be analysed with the perspective it has been said and under which context. As no detail is entirely true, it should be certified by the following statement:

> In regard to some context (*syāt*) it is like this. The only statement one can, therefore, make with certainty is that no description is certain or complete. — Bhandari and Pokharna 2017: 18

When applied to the knowledge one has, Syādavāda defines the limit of the same and, hence, is also known as the principle of contextual perspective. For example: "a man is a father to his son". But this statement does not describe the other relations of the same man. If we say, "he is a good father". Only goodness does not explain all of his attributes and so on. This is the limitation of the language that we can only describe one reality at a time, it depends on which context one is talking about. Hence, every statement becomes partially accurate.

Syādavāda states that even the truth is multiple and relative, and one cannot describe it entirely through the language. In the text, *Pañcāstikāya*, based on the five substances that constitute the cosmos, Ācārya Kundakunda writes:[25]

> The description of the nature of substance is only possible by Saptabhaṅgī Nyāya. According to that, from one point of view, substance is there. From another point of view, it is not there. Perhaps both, i.e. it is and it is not. Perhaps indescribable. Perhaps

---

25 *syādasti nāstubhyam avyaktaṁ punaśca tatrayitayaṁ* ।
dravyaṁ khalu saptabhaṅgamādeśavaśena saṁbhavati ॥
— *Pañcāstikāya* 1.14

> it is and indescribable. Perhaps it is not and indescribable. Perhaps it is, it is not and indescribable. —Jalaj 2016: 28

Hence, the knowledge about the truth stays incomplete at any given time as far as the modes, that are only grasped through the five senses, are concerned. Keeping this statement in mind,

> Syādvāda can be compared with the Gödel's Incompleteness Theorems which postulate that knowledge about the nature of reality has severe limitations. — Bhandari and Pokharna 2017: 18

Hence, the truth can wholly be understood within the ambit of one's experiences and realizations. However, to describe it, one has to take the help of language.

As the human race's quest to seek reality appears to be our innate nature, the principle of Anekāntavāda, helps us understand so. We can dive deeper into the world of knowledge through a relative perspective. The philosophy of Jainism depicts that knowledge can be divided into three categories — "the known, unknown and unknowable" (ibid.: 19). Whereas, we can know the unknown through seeking about it, the unknowable cannot be known, as far as sensory organs and the mind are concerned. Blending these three aspects of knowledge about a specific object, i.e. "the known, unknown and unknowable", takes the seeker to seven states of affirmation known as Saptabhaṅgī. "The modern concepts of statistics and probability are incorporated in these seven possibilities" (Idib.: 19). It is incredible to realize that only seven descriptions can be made to know whatever there is about a specific object, situation or persona. Accordingly, we analyse how constricted our way of understanding the truth is.

Nayavāda (The Theory of Different Standpoints)

Analysis of Anekāntavāda leads one to realize that it must have been evolved from Nayavāda,

> which can be defined as a perspective from different standpoints. It is based on the fact that all objects in the Universe possess a large number of modes of existence (*paryāya*).
>
> — Bhandari and Pokhsna 2017: 25

At any given time one can only perceive a specific thing or situation from any one of the following standpoints or modes; as mentioned in the text on reality by Ācārya Umāsvāti:[26]

> The philosophical standpoints are: the common person's view, generic view, practical view, linear view, literal view, etymological view and actuality view. — Tatia 2011: 23

It is mesmerizing how the view changes from shallow to deep after gaining knowledge about a particular subject or object. These seven viewpoints help one understand the details of an object as described below:

> The first standpoint, the common person's view, overlooks the distinction between the remote and the immediate, noting one or the other as if it were the whole, depending upon the intention of the observer. — Ibid.: 24

For example, two people are discussing a topic that has little to do with the third person entering the room. As soon as one of them takes the third one's name in some context and as the third one has some presumptions about the already sitting people in the room, he assumes that they are gossiping about him. he gets annoyed and leaves the room immediately. In this situation, the third person only noticed the immediate situation and did not even try to analyse the gist of the discussion. We find many people like these in our daily lives. Meanwhile, the same person becomes mature with time and laughs at his previous actions when he analyses the whole scenario.

> The second standpoint, the generic view, combines the part with the whole. — Tatia 2011: 24

---

26 *naigama-saṁgraha-vyavahāra-ṛjuśruta-śabda-samabhirudh-aivambhūtā nayaḥ* ॥ — *Tattvārthasūtra* 1.33

It is evident by the meaning of the word generic, which means "applicable to an entire class or group". The generic view sees the situation or substance as a whole without focusing on its specific characteristics. For example, each human being is a part of the human race in general terms. However, each has its own individual, specific traits.

> The third standpoint, the practical view, concentrates on the function of a thing or being. It is analytic in approach and often uses metaphors to explain the nature of things. — Ibid.

Diving deeper into the pool of understanding, this viewpoint pays attention to the unique features of an object and uses similes to define the same. For example, a poet uses the description of the beauty of a woman as an analogy to express the beauty of the moon.

> The fourth standpoint, the linear view, considers as real only those modes which exist at the moment. — Ibid.

Often, we say, "the past has already gone, the future has not arrived yet, hence live in the present". This viewpoint concentrates on the present and tries to solve the dilemma about reality.

> The fifth standpoint, the literal view, uses words at their exact face value to signify the real nature of things. — Ibid.

Hence, it is necessary to grasp the real meaning of words on the path of knowledge and one must not try to change or modify them. But, often in our daily lives, we use many words, the meanings of which have lost their true essence in our vocabularies. For example, one can observe many newly-made temples, publicized as the ancient ones in current times. However, the learned ones speak less and use the words wisely, for they know the importance of the real meanings of words.

> The sixth standpoint, the etymological view, discards the conventional use of a word in favour of the meaning derived from its root. The etymological view asserts that, because the roots of

> synonyms are different, they are not actually "synonyms" in the sense of words that mean the same as each other.
>
> — Tatia 2011: 24

Each synonym of a particular word has a different meaning and origin. Synonyms only describe a nearby idea of a specific word, which is often entirely different from the original word. Hence, the etymological viewpoint takes us towards a deeper understanding of the words and, eventually, through them, towards knowledge.

> The seventh standpoint, the actuality view, recognizes only the action implied by the root-meaning of a word. To be real, the object must satisfy the activity meant by the word.
>
> — Ibid.: 24-25

For example,

> from the actuality view, we would reject jungle and wilderness but accept "woods", "forest" and "the wild" as all describing some actual reality in that area which does support the activities of being wood, being outdoors and being wild. — Ibid.: 26

Similarly, we would reject the authenticity of "turtle" being slow, as the word "turtle" does not depict the speed of the turtle, but the word "slow" depicts it; in this way, a turtle should be called "slow-pacer", but again that would not describe its other traits, at least not in our understanding.

Besides the above seven viewpoints, which help us understand an object's minutes, there are two more *naya*s to be understood in a different context: the transcendental and practical viewpoints. They are called as *niścaya naya* and *vyavahāra naya*. *Niścaya naya* is the higher level of truth, the transcendental or absolute viewpoint, where every object is seen in its unmodified form. When there is no substratum, the substance is seen beyond the boundaries of cause and effect.

Whereas *vyavahāra naya*, also known as the empirical viewpoint, is comparatively the lower level of truth; it is generally known as the practical viewpoint. Hence, the practical viewpoint is relative and explains things in a relative way. For example, the big black bee is black. In this example, the describing words "big" and "black" indicate a relative approach as one's definition of them may vary in comparison to the other. Even the image of the bee in their minds would also be somewhat different. Another example can be of a gold vessel — from the metaphysical point of view, the vessel is not a vessel but gold; from the relative point of view, it is a vessel made up of gold. Both these statements are true in light of the fact that with respect to the vessel, gold is the substance, and the vessel is its mode. Just as in a necklace or a bangle, the substance "gold" stays the same; however, its modes change.

Thus, we analyse that to have a clearer perspective about the truth, it is not only fundamental but also absolutely necessary to understand the coexistence of both the *nayas*. As in all circumstances, we deal with both the realities; where one is the transcendental phenomenon, the other is only one of its infinite modes which are momentary and evolving incessantly.

The *nayas* help us understand the theory of Anekāntavāda better. The doctrine of *naya* depicts:

> There are many partial perspectives from which reality can be determined, none of which is, taken by itself, wholly true but each of which is partially so.[27]

Nayas help us simplify the process of understanding a specific object, situation, personality and, eventually, reality. The process begins with

> an overall picture of the object, then breaks it down into its component parts, which consist of innate qualities and the way the object is perceived and described by the observer.
>
> — Mardia and Rankin 2013: 50

---

27 "Jain Philosophy", Britannica.com, 2021, <https://www.britannica.com/topic/Indian-philosophy/Jain-philosophy> (accessed on 19 July 2021).

For example, meeting someone for the first time only tells us about the general features of his persona. However, spending more time with the same person exposes his different qualities and weaknesses in front of us. Despite all the observations, in reality, each is an individual consciousness on its own individual journey.

Nayavāda and Karma

These theories, at last, guide us to decode the eternal truth. In the context of beginningless relationship of *karma* with the soul, Nayavāda is described beautifully by Ācārya Kundakunda:[28]

> The statement that the space points of kārmic molecules pervade the space points of the soul, or that they touch the soul, has been made from the empirical point of view (*vyavahāra naya*). From the transcendental point of view (*niścaya naya*), the soul neither gets bonded with nor touched by the kārmic matter. — Jain 1994: 67

It is the viewpoint from which the relationship of the soul with the kārmic matter is seen. In a general way, we say that the soul has been bound with *karma* since time immemorial, whereas in a transcendental way, the soul is considered to be omniscient at all times, which keeps bound with the infinite layers of *karma*, which needs to be removed in order to get acquainted with its true nature.

Mankind's pursuit of peeping into reality through philosophy leads it to enquire about the smallest indivisible part of space, time, matter and consciousness. If we try to find out the origin of Anekāntavāda as a concept,

> it can be traced back to the fundamental Jaina doctrine that everything in the universe, except soul (*ātmā*) and *paramāṇu*, is an aggregate (*skandha*), consisting of two or more constituents.
> — Bhandari and Pokharna 2017: 19

---

[28] *jīve kammaṁ baddhaṁ puṭṭhaṁ cedi vavahāranayabhaṇidaṁ* ।
śuddhanayassa du jīve abaddhapuṭṭhaṁ havadi kammaṁ ।।
— *Samayasāra* 141

And what we see in the physical world is not the soul but its manifestations in different forms, which are actually its *karma*.

Two or more atoms cannot only unite through many different ways, but they also display numerous properties, at separate times, under different circumstances, leading to countless observable attributes of consciousness. However, consciousness stays intact in its purest form at all times.

> But when the soul becomes impure by combining with *karma* particles, it becomes *jīva* (living being) which can take many forms, depending on the state of *karmas*. — Ibid.

The beauty of each living being is that, at the core, it is not only the pure soul but also has its individuality. It gets different bodies, various circumstances, relationships, etc; because of the *karma* it has accumulated in the past, and its present actions lay a foundation for its future journey. This way, the *jīva* is bound to the cycle of cause and effect.

Anekāntavāda and Truth

Indian tradition teaches us that a seeker must seek the truth with absolute humility, as it is a multisided phenomenon with various facets that are impossible to understand simultaneously, especially by a layman. However, by studying the theory of Anekāntavāda, we develop a broader perspective that decodes the truth through various points of view. This conveys that no matter, how rude, unfair or cruel one's circumstances appear, they have the elements of wisdom and an underlying pattern. However, we tend to grasp the same through the best of our rational and analytical faculties.

> We perceive things differently, according to our experience and level of understanding, our cultural background and indeed our species. — Mardia and Rankin 2013: 47

For example, interviewing a criminal hated by everybody may bring out the truth about his behaviour, which may have been caused by his unfair surroundings, and we may conclude that he is not a bad person at all.

Sometimes, the picture presented in front of the world can be twisted or manipulated. In current times, the spread of negativity by the media (newspapers, television and social media) depicts the world as if it would soon come to an end and there is no hope. In this context, when one talks to the Non-Resident Indians (NRIs) about what they think of coming back to India, they reply, "The news we see and hear is so scary that we cannot even think of coming back as India seems to be unsafe". But, of course, this statement has only a tiny element of truth, which is valid for all countries.

We are conscious beings on our individual journeys; each of us has a unique purpose, in the form of exceptional talents. But only a few of us are aware of it and even rare are those who work each moment of their lives to live by that. In the context of understanding reality, "every viewpoint is part of the spiritual journey of all souls and is worthy of consideration" (ibid.: 47). Each viewpoint together make a bigger picture, a clearer understanding, eventually laying the foundation of a better psyche and the world. In this context, one may assume that the pursuit towards the truth not only awakens one but also broadens one's viewpoint, where one's level of acceptance towards different processes is enhanced. Where black is not always black, just like white is not the same at all times.

Irrespective of how undeveloped they are, all beings are, in some contexts, equal and, in some, unequal. They are equal in the sense that each is the manifestation of the same life principle due to which they exist, known as the *jīva* (soul). They are unequal because each is embodied differently in their respective kārmic bodies with their individual kārmic baggage. However,

> all life forms have the same purpose, the movement towards *mokṣa*.
> — Mardia and Rankin 2013: 87-88

Similarly,

> each life form is at a different stage on the journey of spiritual evolution, with some more evolved than others in their capacity for reason and insight. — Ibid.: 88

Hence, only by having a pluralistic approach one can understand the complete jigsaw of life. Anekāntavāda provides the base for this approach astonishingly. It leaves one at a place with unlimited horizons where every thought, idea or persona is welcomed.

No matter if one is a crook or a saint, each one, despite being unaware, is searching for his own truth either through happiness or through woes. A few people have a more significant and far-headed perspective to analyse life's situations, whereas most people are caught in a constricted mindset. However, everyone is right in their pursuit in some way or the other.

> The concept of many-sidedness reminds us that each living being has its own limited but valid version of the truth that contributes to the sum total of knowledge of the universe. — Ibid.: 160

Such an approach helps us decode the truth, our surroundings and the people in different circumstances, be they relationships, occurrences or any other favourable or unfavourable incidents. When one's understanding reaches where the layers of the truth start to peel off, one starts to see the bigger, better picture, leading one towards spiritual upliftment.

Language is like a mother that helps us express ourselves. We gain knowledge, understand things, ponder their meanings. But, "entire language can only express a few aspects of truth" (Mahaprajna 2003: 148). No matter how efficient one is with a specific language, one can only express a few thousand traits of truth or anything else, beyond which lies only realization. Hence, the truth can only be experienced and cannot be conveyed through any means.

The theory of Anekāntavāda strengthens the belief that everything is transient because its modes are continuously changing; hence, we cannot describe it with precision at any given time. If we talk about the continuity in the cosmos and how transformation happens, we analyse that at a micro level, creation and destruction are happening incessantly, which cause change in the non-living matter, be it an object or the human body. However, there remains an underlying permanence between the creation of the new mode and the destruction of the same because even creation is not new, just as destruction.

> Origination and destruction become the causes for the transformation and permanence is their underlying concomitance.
>
> — Ibid.: 159

> Hence, nothing new actually happens in the universe.

> Permanence gives origination and destruction a certain order, but does not let any fundamental change take place in reality or existence. — Ibid.: 160

While studying philosophy, we observe that the core nature of the substance remains the same. Because a substance cannot leave its innate attributes under any circumstance at any point in time.

Language has severe limitations in depicting and understanding a concept. In the context of reality, Lord Mahāvīra said:

> He who says that truth exists and he who denies its existence are both incorrect. They can only be right in a relative sense.
>
> — Mahaprajna 2013: 47

In our pursuit of truth, we often tend to fall into endless arguments; in such a scenario, silence plays a vital role. As one's level of knowledge increases, so does one's ability to speak less to avoid arguments. As

> he, who knows the absolute, cannot and does not speak. For, whatever we speak is bound to be incomplete and therefore controversial. — Ibid.

Hence, non-absolutism prevents us from indulging in useless arguments and teaches us to peep in and recognize the strength of silence and how important it is to use the words we utter wisely.

Comparison with the Theory of Relativity

Often, people can be seen comparing Anekāntavāda with Albert Einstein's theory of relativity, which is not right as a deeper study of Anekāntavāda shows that it has its roots much before, and the meaning is way ahead than the theory of relativity. Hence, the latter can be a smaller part of Anekāntavāda but not the whole theory itself.

> In the Special Theory of Relativity (STR) the parameters of motion of an object (velocity, time, spatial dimensions) depend on the frame of reference of the observer and the object, their motion (or acceleration) is relative to each other.
>
> — Bhandari and Pokharna 2017: 26

Hence, when we try to find a similarity between the two, we realize that they match up to a level where it depends on the mindset of the observer while observing and deciding about a specific object or circumstance. We notice that "in STR, time and space (and motion) are not absolute, so does in Anekānta" (ibid.). Anekāntavāda is also compared with relativism which defines itself :

> There is no absolute truth, only the truths that a particular individual or culture happen to believe.[29]

Whereas Anekāntavāda says, the absolute truth can only be known in its entirety through realization, but it becomes relative as soon as it is described through words.

Anekāntavāda is the main principle that states that everything in the universe has multiple aspects. It can also be understood as

---

29 "Relativism". vocabulary.com, 2021, <https://www.vocabulary.com/dictionary/relativism#:~:text=Relativism%20is%20the%20belief%20that,about%20what's%20moral%20and%20immoral.> (accessed on 28 July 2021).

the presence of infinite attributes in an object simultaneously, some of which can even be opposite and contradictory.

Anekāntavāda and the Uncertainty Principle

A fragment of Anekāntavāda can be compared to the modern-day uncertainty principle as the latter, too, depicts the limits of our speculations. Werner Heisenberg's uncertainty principle is about the limitations of the possibilities of knowing. The principle states:

> There is a fundamental limit to what we can know about the behaviour of the smallest scales of nature. Where the most we can hope for is to calculate probabilities for where things are and how they will behave.[30]

Hence, as per the principle of uncertainty, immense possibilities remain to probe further even after having an assumption that we know it all and so does in Anekāntavāda. For example, when we try to measure the activities of an electron in terms of its velocity and position without modifying it, even with the best apparatus, it remains impossible to assess the two, together. Scientist and author Michio Kaku depicts the Heisenberg's uncertainty principle in the following way:

> We can never know the exact position and velocity of a single electron simultaneously, no matter how sensitive our measuring devices are. We can know one condition or the other, but not both at the same time. — Kaku and Thompson 1995: 43

According to Heisenberg, a single electron can be tracked down only in probabilities in terms of its behaviour; however, the behaviour of the set of electrons can be predicted with the help of the uncertainty principle.

---

30 Jha, Alok. What is Heisenberg's Uncertainty Principle? *Theguardian.com.* (accessed on 29 July 2021). <https://www.theguardian.com/science/2013/nov/10/what-is-heisenbergs-uncertainty-principle>

> In the subatomic realm, only probabilities can be calculated. It is impossible to know the exact position and velocity of an electron, it is impossible to predict much about the electron's individual behaviour. We can, however, predict with amazing accuracy the probability that a large quantity of electrons will behave a certain way. — Ibid.: 44

We need not mention that even an electron has more attributes other than velocity and position, which constantly change.

A simpler example of the uncertainty principle is that Central Board of Secondary Education (CBSE) exams are held yearly in India and over 28 lakh[31] (over 2.8 million) students took the exam in 2018. It is difficult to predict a single student's performance, but the board can determine, with accuracy, the average performance of the students from the entire country. This way we can have the probability about how millions of students will perform in the exam even before they go through it but find ourselves unable to predict an individual student's result.

In the context of human behaviour, one may say that each thought and action first occurs at a subatomic level, and factors like intent, destiny and free will lay out their future plan. However, uncertainty is always there about what will happen in the near or distant future. For example, not all leaders are good and not all good leaders were always worthy and also no one can predict if an average leader today turns out to be a great one in future. Probabilities are always there.

In his book, *The Logic of Scientific Discovery* (1968), Karl Popper expresses:

---

31 Over 28 lakh students to appear for CBSE Class 10, Class 12 Board Exam 2018: Important instructions to keep in mind. Indiatoday.in, *India Today*, 2018, <https://www.indiatoday.in/education-today/news/story/over-28-lakh-students-to-appear-for-cbse-class-10-class-12-board-exam-2018-important-instructions-to-keep-in-mind-1182046-2018-03-05> (accessed on 4 August 2021).

> There can be no "absolutely true" scientific laws because our understanding is constantly developing and shifting.
>
> — Mardia and Rankin 2013: 56-57

Like free will, even in the universe there are always multiple sets of possibilities, out of which, only one can happen at once. This can be termed as the free will of the universe. This leaves us at a point where everything, every thought, every subject and every object become incomplete, relative, interlinked and philosophical. And we get inspiration to

> not repudiating previously established truths, but either enlarging upon or refining them. The many-sided nature of truth gives it its strength and indeed its sacred character.
>
> — Ibid.: 48

Which, irrespective of (sometimes) appearing harsh, is spiritual and keeps us on the track of seeking newer and fresher horizons every moment.

2

Science in Jainism

Beyond *man's innumerable quests, failures and successes to know the universe and its workings, the eternal truth stays untouched and unexplored.*

In our daily lives, we are acquainted with science as a rational subject that can prove something through an experiment. Hence, it is a favourite subject of many, who believe in logic and are curious to know about how things work.

> Science is a systematic enterprise that builds and organizes knowledge in the form of testable explanations and predictions about the universe.[1]

However, through our experiences and observations, we admit that irrespective of the numerous growths scientific developments have made, science has severe limitations and there are innumerable occurrences in the world which cannot be described logically but can only be experienced by one.

Each of us is aware of the vastness of the subject of the universe and perhaps no one can understand its fullness through one paper or book or, in a lifetime and, to be precise, in many lifetimes. Only

---

1 "Science", wikipedia.com, 2021. <www.wikipedia.org/wiki/science> (accessed on 6 August 2021).

a fraction can be covered, can be thrown light upon, that too with a certain, specific perspective. Though we will agree upon,

> before the universe was created, there was *dharma* (laws). There is nothing universal except the laws of Physics. Nothing is absolute, neither time, nor space, nor properties of matter. Everything depends upon the frame of reference used. — Bhandari 2015: 96

Absolutism exists; however, no matter how efficiently the words are used, it cannot be described through them; it can only be realized by one's intellect.

Science is a reality that enacts under specific eternal, universal laws which are, "objective, applicable everywhere, at all times and govern all processes involving matter" (ibid.). A philosophical approach towards science indicates that not only matter but it also includes abstract phenomena like consciousness, the workings of which fall into the ambit of the laws of the universe. And only these laws appear to be the sole supreme that runs the cosmos. When we talk about Jaina philosophy, we analyse that it does not talk about a supreme power that runs the universe.

> Both Jainism and Science do not subscribe to miracles. Thus, Jainism is quite scientific in its approach. — Ibid.

Whereas science talks about the universality of the non-living (*ajīva*) matter, Jainism, and for that matter any religious philosophy, talks about the objectivity of both non-living and the living (*jīva*), simultaneously. Both of them, i.e. non-living matter and the consciousness, fall under the category of substance in the philosophy of Jainism.

Contemplation about science displays some topics: substance — from which the universe is made, cosmology — the shape of the universe and if it has a beginning or an end, space–time — under and through which things change their modes, and metaphysics — that includes the rest of the phenomenon about reality. Let us now analyse what Jaina philosophy says about these topics.

Dravya (Substance)

Ācārya Umāsvāti mentions in his text on reality titled *Tattvārthasūtra*,[2] "the media of motion and of rest, space and matter are extended non-sentient entities" (Tatia 2011: 123). He also describes,[3] "these entities are substances. Souls are also substances" (ibid.). Interestingly, in Jaina philosophy even the soul has been put under the category of substances that constitute the universe. And not only the soul substance is eternal but also the rest of the five substances are eternal and self-sustained, which means all the substances are neither created by a supreme being nor they can be destroyed.

The beauty of being human is that we are always curious to know about our roots. Our mind is always at work to search, to know, and this quest takes us to many successes. Being the most intellectually developed species on the planet, we are similar in many ways; this is why two people in different parts of the world may discover the same thing and have similar experiences and realizations. When we talk about the smallest indivisible part of matter, we can gratefully remember the Greek philosophers.

> Since the time of Greeks, scientists have assumed that the building blocks of the universe were tiny point particles. Democritus coined the word atomos to describe these ultimate, indestructible units of matter. — Kaku and Thompson 1995: 4

The uniqueness of Jaina philosophy lies in what it considers as substance. According to it, the universe mainly comprises of two substances: the living substance called *jīva* and the non-living substance called *ajīva*. Both of these substances are eternal and self-existing. The *ajīva* consists of five substances, viz.:

1. *pudgala* (matter),
2. *ākāśa* (space), which is further subdivided into two parts:

---

[2] *ajīvakāyā-dharmā-dharmā-kāśa-pudgalāḥ* । — *Tattvārthasūtra* 5.1

[3] *dravyāṇi jīvāś ca* । — Ibid. 5.2

lokākāśa (finite cosmic space) where all the six substances reside, and *alokākāśa* (infinite supracosmic space), which starts beyond the boundaries of the cosmic space,

3. *dharmāstikāya* (medium of motion),
4. *adharmāstikāya* (medium of rest), and
5. *kāla* (time), which is again subdivided into two parts, viz. *niścaya kāla*, the absolute time, and *vyavahāra kāla*, the practical time, through which we measure different events of our lives.

The existence of three non-living substances is established. However, *dharmāstikāya* and *adharmāstikāya* could not be proven experimentally.

A German Indologist and researcher of Jainism Walther Schubring[4] (1881–1969) wrote in one of his books:

> The five fundamental facts, all share in eternity. The space embraces both the world (*loka*) and the non-world (*aloka*), whereas the remaining four are concerned with the expansion of the world (*loka*).
>
> — 2000: 126

Loka (cosmic space) can further be subdivided into three parts for our understanding — *madhya loka* (middle world or the horizontal dimension) where all humans, animals, stars, planets, suns and moons are located, *adholoka* (downward dimension or the hells) where the infernal beings reside and *ūrdhvaloka* (upward dimension or the heavens) where the divine beings are located.

Interestingly, *ajīva* (non-living substances), "with the single exception of matter, all are immaterial (*arūpa*)" (ibid.: 8). Which means only the *pudgala* substance has a form and is detectable. The smallest, indivisible unit of *pudgala* substance is known as the *paramāṇu* (absolute atom):

---

4 Walther Schubring, <https://second.wiki/wiki/walther_schubring> (accessed on 12 August 2021).

> The smallest particle of matter consists of only one unit of matter and is a conglomerate of the qualities of colour, taste, smell and touch.
> — Tatia 2011: 123

Whereas, when it comes to the rest of the non-living substances like the medium of motion, rest and space,

> even though they fill the world (cosmic space) completely, they are, in fact, as little palpable as are the flames of a thousand candles lighting a closed room.
> — Schubring 2000: 127

Interestingly, time (*kāla*), despite being included in the six substances, does not have a being (*asti*) and hence does not possess a *kāyā* (extended body) or occupy any space point; it is that abstract phenomenon which we use to live our lives practically. Hence, the five substances having an *asti* (*astitva* or beingness) and extension together are called *pañcāstikāya*.

When it comes to the two unique substances that help neutrally in movement and halt, we may ponder how water works as a medium of motion and also of rest for a fish. "Coming and going, speaking, moving an eyelid, activity of the inner sense, speech and body" and on the other "standing motionless, sitting, lying, confinement to the activity of the inner sense" (ibid.), each action as well as inaction falls into the ambit of these two substances, *dharma* and *adharma*. Indeed, these are unique and exciting features of the Jaina philosophy. They not only enhance the contemplation about substances further but also provide a wide base for research in scientific as well as philosophical fields.

Six Universal Qualities of a Substance

There are six universal qualities common in all substances — "*astitva, vastutva, dravyatva, prameyatva, pradeśatva* and *agurulaghutva*".[5] These can be translated as: "being, entityhood, substancehood,

---

[5] Jain Philosophy (2) 14 — Shad Dravya (Six Universal Substances), Jainsite.com, <https://jainsite.com/jainism_post/jain philosophy-2-14-shad-dravya/> (accessed on 15 August 2021).

objectivity, possession of space-points and eternal persistence" (Mahendra Kumar 2010: 117), respectively.

Understanding these six traits further, "being" implies incessant existence; a specific substance neither loses its individuality nor meets extinction due to this quality. Entityhood signifies that the substance is able to be bound in the cycle of cause and effect.

> Substancehood means the characteristic of being a substratum of qualities and modes. Objectivity means the possibility of becoming an object of knowledge. Possession of space-points indicates that the substance occupies space in its various modes. *Agurulaghutva* (eternal persistence) signifies the quality of abiding to its own nature. — Ibid.

Basically, each substance continues to have these six characteristics independent of the transformations it goes through in the progression of time. "*Agurulaghutvam* is precisely the quality which prevents a substance from surrendering its substancehood" (ibid.). Despite being philosophical, these concepts are aesthetic.

Pudgala (Matter) in Jaina Philosophy

> *Oh humans! to know the truth, thy have to differentiate between thyself and the matter. For thy share the closest bond with the same, and in the art of differentiating lies* liberation.

We notice the physicality of matter at all times around us, in each of our chores, as "material substance constitutes the observable universe and, together with energy, forms the basis of all objective phenomena".[6] However, philosophers aim to break down an object to find its building blocks to know how things work. In this context, Jaina philosophers named matter as *pudgala* and have defined the same as "that which has the innate nature of association and dissociation, such corporeal inert substance is *pudgala*" (Varni 2014a: 67). Most of us wake up with an alarm every morning, freshen

---

6 "Matter." *Britannica.com*. Web. 23 December 2022. <www.britannica.com/science/matter>

up, have tea/coffee and prepare ourselves for the day. During each of the doing, be it as an individual or at a collective level; we use objects which join and get separated all along. For example, in the action of brushing our teeth, the association of toothpaste, brush and water happen with our teeth, and after completing that task, they part ways. Similar happenings of alliance and separation keep taking place throughout one's personal life and with everyone around.

These acts of union and dissolution are possible because, at a subtler level, the tiniest part of matter has this innate ability; this is the materiality of matter. In the philosophical text *Tattvārthasūtra*, Ācārya Umāsvāti describes the nature of *pudgala*[7] further, "the clusters of matter and single atoms have material qualities" (Tatia 2011: 124). To understand the same better, we can say that the material nature of (absolute) atom reflects in the bunches of matter. For example, a single grain of an uncooked lentil cannot be located if fallen on the ground, whereas it becomes easier to find the same if there are many. However, we observe that a single grain has the same taste and qualities as the group of grains (of the same lentil), due to which the specific flavour of that lentil is possible. Hence, one can grasp it either way from many numbers of grains to a single grain or from a single grain to many grains. In philosophy, we take the single grain, or the absolute atom, to understand the nature of things. Hence, we see that the existence of *paramāṇu* can be inferred on observation of their collective effect" (Sikdar 1978: 203).

In the context of *pudgala* (matter), when we try to find out the number of units in an object, Umāsvāti explains,[8] "the number of units in clusters of matter may be numerable, innumerable or infinite" (Tatia 2011: 126). In the above example of a lentil, once it is cooked, it becomes hard to know how many grains it contains. This uncertainty increases with the quantity of the cooked lentil;

---

7 *rūpiṇaḥ pudgalāḥ* | — *Tattvārthasūtra* 5.4

8 *saṁkhyeyāsaṁkhyeyāś ca pudgalānām* | — Ibid. 5.10

for example, when the same lentil gets cooked in a household, the units of the lentil can be counted or the number can be guessed. But when the same gets cooked at a charity kitchen where thousands of people are eating, and the lentil is in the process of getting cooked continuously, it becomes difficult to count the exact number of units. (PS: This is a simple daily-life example just to have an idea of the philosophical nature of matter; in an absolute sense, it does not apply on the same.)

Types of Pudgala

Maman, why cannot one rejoin the broken branch with its tree?
On the contrary, why does milk re-unites with its contemporaries?
Why cannot one capture one's own shadow?
Do words have a physical existence
Or are they merely philosophical?
Why is one born to one's parents only?
Is there a science behind everything
Or everything exists casually?

Now come the queries that any curious mind can and must have. Let us look around and observe some daily life situations, for example, a singer's songs, an actor's acting skills in a movie, a leader's motivational speech and an author's wisdom in the form of a book. All of these stay available on different platforms, in other formats, even after the demise of that specific person. Have we ever noticed how can it be possible? Most of us ponder that our words are conscious; however, they do not seem to be. Dealing with the subject of matter (*pudgala*), Ācārya Kundakunda describes elaboratively in his text *Pañcāstikāya*, written around the second century CE about how wood, water, words, light and darkness, and all subjects that belong to the senses along with those which are even beyond sensory perception like *karma* fall into the category of *pudgala*. Ācārya Kundakunda has divided *pudgala* into six categories, from gross to subtle:

1. Very gross (*bādara-bādara*) — Those objects that do not recombine themselves once separated, e.g. wood and stone.
2. Gross (*bādara*) — Those objects that recombine themselves again even after getting separated, e.g. milk, water, oil and purified butter (*ghee*).
3. Gross-subtle (*bādara-sūkṣma*) — Those material substances that appear gross but cannot be separated or held by hands, e.g. sunlight, shadow and moonlight.
4. Subtle-gross (*sūkṣma-bādara*) — Those substances which are subtle but appear to be gross like touch, taste, smell and word.
5. Subtle (*sūkṣma*) — Those substances which are minute and cannot be grasped through the senses like *karma*.
6. Subtle-subtle (*sūkṣma–sūkṣma*) — Substances that are even subtler than *karma* such as a highly minute aggregate of atoms (*dvayaṇu skandha*).

Seeing the above-detailed description of the gross as well as the minute matter, we notice that even the understanding of matter is more philosophical and less about trying to prove the same on a logical ground. One may think about the material nature of light, darkness, words, etc. When we dive deeper into the metaphysics of life, we notice that consciousness is inevitably bound to express itself through matter and even "life is a manifestation of matter" (Bhatnagar 1984). In Indian philosophy, the body of a being is considered matter that takes shape according to the *karma* of a specific being.

Skandha (Group of Infinite Absolute Atoms) and Molecule

Oh, the building blocks of materiality have been found!
However, being the groups of immeasurable tiny-minies
As the absolute fragment, can they be crowned?

Attributes of *pudgala* have been further described:

> Due to its mutual bonding only different, ordinary and peculiar, objects get produced in the world, which is termed as *skandha*.

> Touch, taste, smell and colour are the prominent attributes of *pudgala*. — Varni 2014b: 67

Skandha can be compared with a molecule, which is a group of two or more atoms that forms the smallest identifiable unit into which a pure substance can be divided and can still retain the composition and chemical properties of the substance.[9] For example, a water molecule starts to own the attributes of water when it becomes touch, taste, smell and colour worthy by the union of two hydrogen atoms and one oxygen atom. When we try to probe even further, we realize that even an atom, be it of hydrogen or oxygen, is made up of electron, proton and neutron, which in turn are made up of quarks as "each proton and each neutron contain three quarks".[10]

Ācārya Kundakunda mentions in the philosophical treaties about matter written in the first century BCE *Pañcāstikāya*[11] that "*skandha* is made up of infinite *paramāṇus*" (Jalaj 2016: 50). Physicists today can peel off the material substance's layers in a beautiful way. However, we notice that there still lies a gateway of possibilities of infinite absolute atoms inside even the tiniest particle. Probing further into decoding the nature of non-living matter, ancient Indian philosophers have indicated that even words result from bilateral abrasion of many such *skandhas*, which means the basic building blocks are the same for words. Because, sound, no matter if it gets shaped through speech or writing, is also *pudgala*. Acārya Kundakunda mentions[12] that a word gets produced due to the mutual friction (contact) of many *skandhas*. Hence, a

9 "Molecule", *Britannica.com*. Web. 23 December 2022. <www.britannica.com/science/molecular-beam>

10 The Atom Builder Guide to Elementary Particles. *Pbs.org*. Web. 25 December 2022. <www.pbs.org/wgbh/aso/tryit/atom/elempartp.html#:~:text=Quarks%20make%20up%20protons%20and, fast%2Dmoving%20point%20of%20energy.>

11 *skaṁdhaḥ paramāṇu saṁgasaṁghātaḥ* । — *Pañcāstikāya* 79

12 *śabdaḥ skaṁdhaprabhavaḥ* । *spr̥ṣṭeṣu teṣu jāyate śabda utpādako niyataḥ* ॥ — Ibid.

word is definitively a product (Jalaj 2016: 50). This way, we analyse that everything that has physicality in the universe has identical foundational God particles, which can only be grasped when they are in *skandha* (groups).

Paramāṇu (the Absolute Atom) in Jaina Philosophy

Look, the main lead is found
The building block of all physicality
The hidden treasure
That seems the farthest
But is the closest
On this realization
The seeker is astounded.

In his search for truth, after peeling off the countless layers of relativity, man eventually reaches a state of the ultimate, where nothing is left afterwards. This is the state of realization when the absolute atom becomes understandable. In Jaina metaphysics, the *pudgala* is a tangible reality and its first form is *paramāṇu* (the absolute atom) (Sikdar 1978). In the *Pañcāstikāya,* which is about the five fundamental substances of the universe with an *asti* (*astitva* or beingness) and extension, Ācārya Kundakunda describes *paramāṇu* as:[13]

> The last outline, the last iota, the ultimate halt of all the *skandhas* is *paramāṇu*. The *paramāṇu* is eternal, which means indestructible in the past, present and future without sound, occupies only one Space-point and is monolithic. — Jalaj 2016: 49

Being the most fundamental building block of the material world, the *paramāṇu* is perpetual, which indicates that it never loses its essence, no matter how much effort is made to destroy it. Ācārya Kundakunda also clarifies,[14] "the *paramāṇu* is devoid of sound itself;

---

[13] *sarveṣāṁ skaṁdhānāṁ yoantyastaṁ vijānīhi paramāṇu* ।
sa śāśvatoaśabdaḥ ekoavibhāgi mūrtibhavaḥ ॥ — *Pañcāstikāya* 77

[14] *sa jñeyaḥ paramāṇuḥ pariṇāmaguṇaḥ svayamaśabdaḥ* ।
— Ibid. 78

however, it is the cause of the word" (Jalaj 2016: 49). To elaborate, we can say that the absolute atom does not possess sound. Yet, it is the cause of the same but only when in groups (of many similar counterparts) as it has the ability to generate friction. This situation of the absolute atom is identical to the idiom "it takes two to make a quarrel".

Strengthening the imperishability of the absolute atom again, Ācārya Kundakunda writes:[15] "the *paramāṇu* is eternal, which means it is forever indestructible" (Jalaj 2016: 50). No matter how much chaos is caused, the *paramāṇu* will not lose its existence. As it only sieges one space point of the entire universe, "it is capable, as well as incapable of providing space to others" (ibid.). Describing further how the absolute atom sustains its eternal properties, Ācārya Kundakunda conveys that "due to occupying only one space-point, it keeps its formlessness and similar attributes intact" (ibid.). Now the query arises: where does the absolute atom start occupying space and where does it stop? Ācārya Kundakunda clarifies:

> Because of occupying one space-point only, its beginning, middle and end are all the same. It is indivisible and monolithic. That is why it does not have any scope for anything else. — Ibid.

Another Indian scholar from sometime between the second and fifth century CE, Ācārya Umāsvāti, also confirms the essence of the absolute atom[16] by mentioning in his philosophical treatise, "there are no additional units in an atom" (Tatia 2011: 126). It is individual and self-sufficient in itself. In the absolute sense, the *paramāṇu* seems to be an illusion, but it is not. The beauty of this ancient Indian philosophy is that it explains the unexplainable.

The uniqueness of *paramāṇu* does not stop here:

---

15 *nityo nānāvakāśo na sāvakāśaḥ pradeśato bhettā* ।
skaṁdhānāmapi ca karttā pravibhaktā kālasaṁkhyāyāḥ ॥
— *Pañcāstikāya* 80

16 *na-noḥ* । — *Tattvārthasūtra* 5.11

> Due to the attribute of occupying one space-point, it has the strength to penetrate the *skandha* (molecules) into many pieces.
> —Jalaj 2016: 50

This attribute of the *paramāṇu* is similar to the quality of the neutrino as neutrinos are nearly massless particles that can move as easily through lead as we move through the air and are notoriously difficult to pin down.[17]

Scientist Michio Kaku also writes, "neutrinos leave no traces of their presence; they can easily penetrate through the earth" (1995: 61).

Dealing with the next query that may arise in the readers minds, if the *paramāṇu* can penetrate the *skandha*, how can it make one? Ācārya Kundakunda leaves no stone unturned as he clarifies further:

> It is also the doer of the *skandha*, and due to its potency of union, it produces the molecules. —Jalaj 2016: 50

Indeed the *paramāṇu* is the ultimate particle as it is the one that creates the visible objects in the entire cosmos and it is the one that destroys them.

Just like words (be they are spoken or written) are the products of *pudgala* (non-living matter), we need the help of *pudgala* only to understand the abstract nature of time. For practical purposes, we are supposed to give forms, symbols and units to the concept of time, which is made of non-living matter. Moving ahead, Ācārya Kundakunda throws light upon the involvement of the absolute atom in the same. The teacher mentions,[18] "the *paramāṇu* is the one that divides the time and measures and calculates the numbers"

---

17 Marder, Jenny. What Is a Neutrino ... And Why Do They Matter? *pbs. org*. Web. 25 January 2011. <www.pbs.org/newshour/science/what-is-a-neutrino-and-why-should-anyone-but-a-particle-physicist-care>

18 *pravibhaktā kālasaṁkhyāyāḥ* ı — *Pañcāstikāya* 80

(Jalaj 2016: 50). For it is the building block for everything that is not abstract and we notice that as soon as mathematics enters the numeric dimension, it becomes material. We see that the Jaina metaphysics maintains that *paramāṇu* is both cause (*kāraṇa*) and effect (*kārya*) of the material world.[19]

Matter and Atom in Different Philosophies

> *Oh child! strive to know the matter in totality to know thy immortality.*

Ancient Indian scientists, scholars and philosophers were all naturalists as they aimed at finding the secrets of nature. Interestingly, they used to follow a strict regimen in their lifestyle as well, which used to be in sync with the laws of the cosmos. Hence, in India, they were known as saints, *ṛṣis*, *muni*s and *ācāryas*. Kaṇāda Ṛṣi, the founder of the Vaiśeṣika school of Indian philosophy, was one such natural scientist and philosopher who formulated the theory of atoms 2,500 years before John Dalton's discovery.[20] He considered the atom indivisible, a point source and without magnitude (Bhatnagar 1984).

The change first has to occur at a substantial level to observe the visible difference. However, at the most minute level, where the absolute atoms exist, there is an unchangeable essence, which does not change at all. The view of Nyāya-Vaiśeṣika is that "the atom, as the basis of changes in all material substance, exists as absolutely permanent without any kind of change" (Sikdar 1978).

Kapila Muni founded the Sāṁkhya school of thought in the first

---

19 Sikdar, J.C., 1970, "Jaina Atomic Theory", *Physical Concepts*, 5(2): 199-218.

20 Bhattacharya, Shantanu. Sage who dreamed of the Atom. *Santanub.medium.com*. 10 March 2021. Web. 16 November 2022. <https://santanub.medium.com/the-sage-who-dreamed-of-atom-7021d5dd73f#:~:text=Acharya%20Kanada%2C%20also%20known%20as,epitomized%20the%20earliest%20Indian%20physics.>

millennium BCE.[21] *Prakṛti* of the Sāṁkhya school represents Matrix or Primordial Matter as non-living, eternal, infinite, all-pervading, undecaying and indestructible in nature (Sikdar 1978: Intro.). In contrast, *puruṣa* is the principle of being the indifferent spectator of the changes that take place in *prakṛti* (Basu, Major B.D. 1915: Preface). This way, the Sāṁkhya philosophy depicts *prakṛti* as the non-living matter and *puruṣa* as the living substance of the universe.

Interestingly, all Indian schools of philosophy convey more or less the same truth. In the context of matter and atom, some schools tally on some points while disagreed on some. For example, the Buddhist tradition advocates atomism like the Nyāya-Vaiśeṣika and the Jaina systems of thought (Sikdar 1978). From the fourth to fifth century CE,[22] Buddhist philosopher and Vasubandhu explained that the nature of the atom (*paramāṇu*) is to exist as combined (Sikdar 1978). Hence, one atom cannot be grasped, whereas a group of innumerable atoms can be seen, touched, smelled, tasted or heard. A group of atoms makes it the object of knowledge that can be accessed through the five senses.

Three Indian schools of thought, viz. Sāṁkhya — Nyāya-Vaiśeṣika and Jaina, agree on one point that self-identity of the fundamental substance as substratum is to remain non-divisible (Sikdar 1978). At the elementary level, we notice that an object has an unchangeable, indestructible and indivisible essence. This makes the smallest unit of matter the subject matter of realization that transcends physicality.

---

21 "Samkhya", 1 January 2023. Web. 13 January 2023. <https://en.wikipedia.org/wiki/Samkhya#:~:text=Sage%20Kapila%20is%20traditionally%20credited%20as%20a%20founder%20of%20the%20Samkhya%20school.>

22 Gold, Jonathan C., "Vasubandhu", *Stanford Encyclopaedia of Philosophy*, Web. 7 January 2021. 15 January 2023, <https://plato.stanford.edu/entries/vasubandhu/>

Absolute Particle, Quantum Mechanics and Supersymmetry

Realizing the fineness of the *paramāṇu*, we conclude that it is the sheer base for the visible world. From gross objects like a box and a table to the subtle ones like sound waves, electricity, darkness and light, it is the *pudgala* substance which rules the world; with the ability of getting transformed from gross to subtle and vice versa.

> It was Einstein who first pointed out that under certain circumstances, even a rock (uranium) can turn into a beam of light (a nuclear detonation). — Kaku and Thompson 1995: 27

This discovery from the famous scientist depicts that the indivisible part of matter is of only one kind and each of its counterparts shares the same attributes for all inanimate objects. It also has the ability to be altered into each possible forms like in the above example from a rock to a beam of radiation and the other way around.

The atom was almost forgotten since it was first used by the Greek philosopher Democritus around 450 BCE.[23] It came back to the limelight again when the British chemist John Dalton revived the early ideas about the atom around 1800.[24] The discovery of the smallest possible unit of matter did not and could not be stopped there when, in 1930, Wolfgang Pauli postulated the existence of the neutrino and, in 1955, Clyde Cowan and Frederick Reines recorded the activity of the neutrinos emitted by a nuclear reactor.[25] Michio Kaku writes:

---

23 "5.2 History of the Atom", Ck12.org, 12 January 2021, <https://www.ck12.org/book/ck-12-physical-science-for-middle-school/section/5.2/> (accessed on 24 August 2021).

24 Ibid.

25 "What is a neutrino?", Scientificamerican.com, 7 September 1999, <https://www.scientificamerican.com/article/what-is-a-neutrino/> (accessed on 24 August 2021).

> Of all the particles in the universe, the neutrino is perhaps the most curious, because it is by far the most elusive. It has no charge, probably has no mass, and is exceedingly hard to detect.
> — Kaku and Thompson 1995: 60

From discovering the atom to the neutrino, how unpredictable the journey has been, there is a definitive possibility for something subtler to be discovered.

Somehow, the uncertainty about the finest particle and its behaviour gave rise to quantum mechanics by different groups of physicists between the mid-1800s and early 1900s.[26] Since then, quantum mechanics has triumphed decisively in every experiment performed by scientists on the subatomic level (ibid.: 46).

However, countless questions remain to be answered, leaving mankind with infinite possibilities. For example, can it be true that

> a table exists only if a consciousness is there to observe it and as Descartes said, "I think therefore I am". — Ibid.

In this statement, the object, the non-living matter, belongs to the world of physicality, which exists irrespective of the observer, whereas the "I am" phrase belongs to the spiritual dimension, which exists irrespective of the material world. Both indicate the two principal substances that constitute the universe, the former belongs to the realm of the non-living matter (*pudgala*) and, the latter, to the conscious substance (*jīva*). A well-known spiritual, teacher and author Eckhart Tolle dismisses René Descartes' finding by writing in his international bestseller, *The Power of Now*:

> Descartes had, in fact, given expression to the most basic error: to equate thinking with Being and identity with thinking. — 2001: 12

Understanding the time cycle, as described in Indian philosophies, along with the theory of *karma*, indicates that the events and

---

26 "History of quantum mechanics", Wikipedia, 12 August 2021, <https://en.wikipedia.org/wiki/History_of_quantum_mechanics> (accessed on 26 August 2021).

occurrences happen in a cyclic pattern, and each soul is bound by that. However, with its free will, each soul can choose to step out of that pattern and, in turn, from the cycle. Not only that, but the cyclic pattern also keeps reaching the zeniths of supersymmetry and superasymmetry. During all this, the cosmos keeps returning each being's actions in the form of kārmic particles. In this context, we observe a symmetry in the workings of the universe, which illustrates that nothing wrong ever happens in the universe. Understanding the *karma* theory in depth helps us understand supersymmetry.

> Perhaps the greatest lesson of the past several decades of physics is that nature does not simply find symmetry a convenient feature in building physical structures, nature absolutely demands it.
>
> — Kaku and Thompson 1995: 194

Karma is the inevitable law of the physical world operated by the faculty of consciousness. Souls have been stuck in the cycle of time through their *karma* since time immemorial. When the cycle reaches supersymmetry, the patterns of beings and their *karma* become smoothest, and as the cycle touches the asymmetrical era, the same patterns start to become rough. The understanding of the absolute takes one to grasp the subtlety and necessity of supersymmetry in order to step out of the time cycle.

Paramāṇu, Pudgala Karma (Material Karma) and Soul as Substances

Emotions, desires, dreams, etc, do not come under the subject field of physical science as they can only be felt by that specific living being and cannot be proven and accessed by any scientific experiment. No one can doubt the existence and degrees of emotions. We have favourable emotions towards some people or beings while negative towards others.

> In contrast with standard physics where one deals with matter in time and space coordinate systems, in Jaina science it is the soul which is to be studied in terms of time, space and matter.
>
> — Mardia and Rankin 2013: 101

As mentioned earlier, all these (time, space, matter and the soul) come into the category of substances that constitute the cosmos. This is the unique and outstanding feature of Jaina philosophy: the soul is also considered a substance, the only one with the distinctive characteristic of being conscious, who can know the rest of the substances.

It is not only beautiful but also highly philosophical that the living and the non-living both fall under the same category as far as the constitution of the cosmos is considered. *Karma* is not something abstract but rather a physical reality in the form of *paramāṇus*. "Kārmic matter on a contaminated soul is a fine matter which has infinite number of *kārmons*" (Mardia and Rankin 2013: 104). Kārmic matter, is the asset and liability a soul has, which inevitably travels with it, no matter where it goes, which form it manifests into in each birth, even after each death and rebirth.

> The nature of soul rests in its intellectual function (*upayoga*, which means knowledge and perception), which by means of will and skill is put to use in all possibilities of intellectual cognition. The matters cause the souls to take possession (*grahaṇa*) of the bodies and to enact bodily functions. — Schubring 2000: 128

Depending on its nature, matter that comes in the form of *karma* inevitably either supports or obstructs the activities of the consciousness. For example, writing this book is materialistic, which eventually keeps the intellectualism of the author satiated. This way, the curiosity to write a book supports the *karma* of writing, giving the scholar a feeling of accomplishment.

> The soul has its characteristics of life including bliss, energy, knowledge and perception elements, *pudgala* has its characteristics of lifelessness, touch, flavour, smell and colour. — Ibid.

The beauty lies in the fact that whatever the soul has to express, it does through *pudgala* (non-living matter) in the form of *karma*, be it through the body, language, dreams or passion. The universe is a beautiful platform to observe the interaction, relation, temporary union and absolute separation between these two — the soul and the matter.

Concept of Space

That which provides space to everything in the cosmos, be it the non-living matter or the consciousness, is the space. As Ācārya Umāsvāti mentions in his philosophical work,[27]

> all four substances (*jīva*, *ajīva*, *dharma* and *adharma*) are contained in cosmic space. — Tatia 2011: 126

In the philosophy of the Jainas, even the space is divided into two parts: *lokākaśa*, i.e. the cosmic space that accommodates all other substances within, and *alokākaśa*, i.e. the supracosmic space, i.e. beyond the cosmic space, in which no substance resides and cannot reside.

According to the *Cambridge Dictionary of Philosophy*, space has been defined as,

> an extended manifold of several dimensions, where the number of dimensions corresponds to the number of variable magnitudes needed to specify a location in the manifold. — Audi 2017: 1010

In the observable world, we live in a three-dimensional universe (of length, width and height) in space, and time is considered as the fourth dimension, as "we are always moving forward through time" (Siegel 2019).

> *Ākāśastikāya* or *ākāśa* is defined as — the substance, which acts as a container of other substances. — Mahendra Kumar 2010: 117

Ākāśa is also considered as *astikāya*, i.e. that has an existence. Having all the six qualities of a substance mentioned above, *ākāśa* is regarded as one of the substances constituting the cosmos.

---

27 *lokākāśe vagāhāḥ* । — *Tattvārthasūtra* 5.12

> From substantial point of view, being a homogeneous continuum, it is one and at the same time an indivisible entity.
>
> — Mahendra Kumar 2010: 118

As it pervades the whole universe perpetually and unanimously, it is indivisible, and all the other substances are located in it. For example, this can be a philosophical query, too: Whenever a needle is inserted into the human body, it becomes possible because the body has space, or we may put the same statement the other way around: that space contains the body.

> From spatial point of view, it is ubiquitous, all-pervading and infinite in extent. Hence, its *pradeśas* (space-points) are infinite in number. From temporal point of view, it is eternal. — Ibid.

Like the rest of the substances, the space, too, has neither a beginning nor an end. Despite being a non-living entity, it is different from the *pudgala*, which means

> from the point of view of nature, it is non-corporeal (*amūrta*) and being devoid of touch, taste, odour and colour and is non-physical too. — Ibid.

Space is an immobile substance; it neither moves on its own nor any other substance can cause movement in it; "it is devoid of motion" (ibid.). And as it is a non-living substance, it "is devoid of consciousness, and hence *ajīva*" (ibid.). This description defines space in all its aspects that describe a substance.

Cosmic and SupraCosmic Space

The Jaina thinkers have divided the space of the universe as cosmic space (*lokākāśa*) and have given the name of supracosmic space (*alokākāśa*) to the space that surrounds the cosmic space, where the prior only occupies a tiny part of the latter. When we enquire deeper into the subject of space, newer and more meaningful definition comes out.

> Void space is called *ākāśa*. It has been acknowledged as a monolithic, incorporeal substance. That can accommodate all the

> substances in itself. Despite it being monolithic, to understand its nature, units known as *pradeśa* (space points or smallest indivisible units of space) are given. Even though it is infinite, all the other substances are situated only in a few intermediary parts; this part of the space is known as *loka* (cosmic space), and the entire space outside is called *aloka* (supracosmic space). Because of the unique ability to accommodate (*avagāhana*), there are infinite–infinite substances located in each of its *pradeśa* (space points). — Varni 2012: 219

Hence, we see that cosmic space is only a small part of the supracosmic space, accommodating all known, unknown and unknowable substances in all their known, unknown and unknowable dimensions. It is finite, compared to the supracosmic space, and infinite, in the viewpoint of the space points it possesses.

> It is in the nature of space to give room (*avagāhana*), to any amount of atoms; but this, of course, applies merely to the space of the world, the space of the non-world being completely void.
> — Schubring 2000: 127

Another query that arises in one's mind is that just like space provides accommodation to all the other substances, is there something that provides a base even to the space? To decode this query, scholar Kamal Chand Sogani clarifies:

> Space is its own base and support and does not call for any other substance to accommodate it; it is evident from the fact that there is no other substance of more vastness than this which may provide room to it. — 2001: 28

Amongst all the substances, the unique grandeur of accommodating all the substances belongs to the space alone.

One also develops a query as to why there is a need to divide the space into two parts. Muni Mahendra Kumar interprets the same:

> The space, cosmic and supracosmic, is a single entity. Only due to the presence of other substances we divide space into two parts.
> — 2010: 119

Beautifully, the universe is the best self-sustained model.

Singularity of Space

To solve the dilemma of whether the space, the medium of motion (*dharma dravya*) and of rest (*adharma dravya*) have some varieties or can be further divided, Walther Schubring writes:

> Both space and motion as well as rest are definitely singular, whereas souls and matter are of infinite variety, and, moreover they alone are active. — 2000: 127

Hence, we notice that the *jīva*, despite owning the trait of being conscious, and *pudgala*, despite lacking the attribute of being conscious, share the unique quality of movement. The whole cosmos is the incessant play of the interaction between these two, where the rest of the substances exist neutrally, without absolute non-interference between the relationship of these two.

> *Akāśa* is that which has infinite space points and is spread universally upwards, downwards and diagonally.
> — Varni 2012: 220

Which means the space is everywhere. Schubring writes further:

> There is but one world (*loka*) and beside it but one non-world (*aloka*). The latter surrounds the world on all sides like a hollow sphere and is out of reach, since beyond the boundaries of the world (the cosmic space) the medium of motion (*dharma dravya*) is absent. — 2000: 204

If we say that space is infinite, this will indicate that all the substances reside everywhere, in every direction, in each dimension, and there are no boundaries at all, which will create the dilemma of the infinity of the universe.

To discriminate and also to understand the difference between the two spaces, medium of motion (*dharma dravya*) and its exact contrary, medium of rest (*adharma dravya*), come into the scenario and indicate that as these two substances are absent there, which help in each movement and rest, of the living and the non-living matter, it becomes impossible to access the supracosmic space. Perhaps this is the only way through which the existence of these two substances, i.e. medium of motion and rest, can be known.

> That which lacks the attribute of consciousness is incorporeal, provides room to all the substances, is all-pervasive, and has been characterized as *ākāśa dravya* (space substance) by the individuals who have perceived reality. — Varni 2012: 220

Ākāśa, despite being non-living itself, provides space to all the possible forms of living beings as well as the entire non-living matter of the universe.

Newton's findings about space were quite close to those of the ancient Indian thinkers. He described:

> The earth and the heavenly bodies are situated in an immovable container, of boundless extent, which exists and has always existed, independently of whether it is observed by perceiving minds or not, and independently of whether it is occupied at any particular space or not. — Mahendra Kumar 2010: 51-52

Relationship among dharma dravya, adharma dravya and ākāśa dravya

In essence, the space in *loka* and *aloka* is one. The difference lies in providing residence to the two substances, *jīva* and *pudgala*, with the help of *dharma dravya* (medium of motion) and *adharma dravya* (medium of rest), where absence of one substance leads to the absence of the rest.

If there is no medium of motion (which will inevitably include the medium of rest), any movement started would not be stopped ever; hence, life would not be possible. If there is no *pudgala dravya* (non-living matter), *jīva* would not be able to perform any action. And, at last, if there will be no *jīva dravya*, the only substance with the attribute of consciousness, there will be absolutely no one to observe, to enquire, to find and eventually to write these words. Here, time, being an entity absolutely devoid of existence, is adopted by the conscious substance for practical purposes only.

The existence of "the space substance (*ākāśa dravya*)" is acceptable worldwide. However, accepting the need for the medium of motion and the medium of rest for the constitution of the universe has the scope of enquiry. Let us now try to understand the requirement of these two substances to sustain the habitable and observable cosmos.

According to Jaina philosophy, the space substance, despite being able to provide a base for the soul substance and the non-living matter, has its limitations. When one ponders the difference between the cosmic space (*loka*) and the supracosmic space (*aloka*), one keeps having this query: how are they different? Why is it not possible for space to assist the motion of the soul substance as well as the non-living substance? Which is the boundary that divides cosmic and supracosmic space? The solution lies in understanding the role of the medium of motion, which inevitably includes the medium of rest, as mentioned above. Also, while studying Jaina philosophy, we see that the habitable universe is finite, systematic and, hence, observable.

> If the space itself acts like ether (medium of motion), then the motion of dynamic objects cannot be checked as space would be infinite and indivisible. Thus, the infinite number of matter and souls would continue to roam about in the infinite space without control. If this were so, their association and appearance as an organized, finite, inhabited universe would be extremely improbable, if not altogether impossible.
>
> — Mahendra Kumar 2010: 122

This would lead to the idea of an unorganized cosmos. At this confusing point, the two substances of the medium of motion and rest come into the scenario and provide the solution. Their presence not only determines the boundary of the cosmic space but also differentiates it from the supracosmic space. Hence, we get to understand the need for these two substances. Ācārya Kundakunda has written in his text *Pañcāstikāya*[28] on the substances:

> The cosmic space, the medium of motion and the medium of rest have the same extension. Hence, these are inseparable, and since each has its own unique qualities, they exhibit oneness as well as separateness. — Jain 2020: 185

This means that all three substances, despite coexisting eternally, sharing the same space points and having the same expansion, have their individual existences.

The logic above also helps one understand the eternality of all six substances. The way all substances cannot survive without the absence of any one substance; the eternality of one substance leads to the eternality of another. Hence, the substance that differentiates between the cosmic and supracosmic space must inevitably be among the six. Time, being an abstract substance with no existence, can be said to be something that "pervades through both the spaces, i.e. cosmic and supracosmic" (Mahendra Kumar 2010: 123).

Hence, we conclude that though space is intricately associated with the workings of mediums of motion and rest, it has an individual identity that is unique in itself and cannot be acquired by any other substance, which is to provide space. The above explanation summarizes the relationship among these three substances, i.e. *dharma dravya*, *adharma dravya* and *ākāśa dravya*.

Time

Time is a highly philosophical, abstract concept to understand, which one has to boggle one's mind or perhaps not use the mind at all. It has plenty of definitions, as observed by many philosophers,

---

28 *dharmādharmākāśānyapṛthagbhūtāni samānaparimāṇāni* ।
pṛthaguplabdhiviśeṣāṇi kurvantyekatvamanayatvaṁ ॥
— *Pañcāstikāya* 5.96

scientists and scholars at different times. One of the many definitions from *Merriam-Webster* is:

> A non-spatial continuum that is measured in terms of events which succeed one another from past through present to future.[29]

It is tough to imagine a substance that does not exist in space but is still used for practical purposes. Plato described time as "a moving image of eternity"; Aristotle explained it as "the number of movements in respect of the before and after" (Audi 2017: 1066). Albert Einstein said, "Time is what prevents everything from happening at once".[30]

In Jaina philosophy, *kāla* (time) is one of the six substances constituting the universe. Though each substance is unique in itself, the uniqueness of time is different from the rest of the substances. And this uniqueness lies in its not existing in space. Ācārya Kundakunda differentiates time from the rest of the substances in his philosophical work *Pañcāstikāya.*[31]

> These — the time (*kāla*), the space (*ākāśa*), the medium of motion (*dharma*), the medium of rest (*adharma*), the matter (*pudgala*) and the souls (*jīva*) – are designated as substances (*dravya*), but the substance of time (*kāla*) does not have the attributes of "body" (*kāyā*).
> — Mahendra Kumar 2010: 196

Time envelopes each happening of the entire known, unknown and unknowable universe in all its dimensions, in all its modes and in

---

29 "Time", Merriam-webster.com, <https://www.merriam-webster.com/dictionary/time> (accessed on 11 September 2021).

30 "Albert Einstein Time Quotes", Pinterest.com, <https://in.pinterest.com/pin/4478267-56691653020/#:~:text=Albert%20Einstein%20Time%20Quotes, everything%20from%20happening%20at%20once> (accessed on 17 September 2021).

31 *ete kālākāśe dharmādharmau ca pudgalā jīvāḥ* ।
labhante dravyasaṁjñām kālasya tu nāsti kāyatvaṁ ।।
– *Pañcāstikāya* 6.102

all its attributes. Time can be called the sole spectator of everything through which events happen, from past to present, towards the future. The famous scholar of Jaina philosophy, Jinendra Varni, describes the smallest indivisible unit of time as

> time taken by a *paramāṇu* to travel, with its minimum speed, to its adjoining *paramāṇu*, is *samaya*. — 2012: 327

Here, *samaya* indicates the smallest indivisible unit of time and, as we read above, *paramāṇu* is the smallest indivisible part of matter.

This description of time (*samaya*) also gives rise to the understanding of the concept of space–time. Where to understand one, we inevitably have to understand the other. For example, with the three dimensions of space (length, width and height), we have to consider time as the fourth dimension. However, to understand time, we need to consider at least one dimension of space.

Also, "the minimum period of a particular attribute of all substances is one *samaya*" (Varni 2012: 327). This means any given substance can possess any attribute for at least one *samaya*. The time gives change its existence as the beginning of a change starts from the smallest indivisible unit of time. Passing through one *samaya* only, any incident, any change, in any substance, is possible.

Practical time and Transcendental Time (vyavahāra kāla and niścaya kāla)

Each happening can be segregated into two parts: the first can be seen and observed through our senses and mind. In contrast, the second occurs at the minute level, which, despite causing that specific happening, cannot be seen or observed, well, at least not through the senses. These two are the practical and the metaphysical happenings, respectively. When put under the lens of time, we call it the practical time and transcendental time or *vyavahāra kāla* and *niścaya kāla*. In Jaina philosophy,

> *kāla* usually means a period of time of some length, of which *samaya* is the ultimate indivisible unit. But, in common parlance, the word *samaya* is indicative of *kāla*.
>
> — Mahendra Kumar 2010: 124

Hence, we can say that *kāla* is the practical time and *samaya* is the transcendental or metaphysical time.

Among all six substances, the uniqueness of *kāla* is that it does not have an *asti* (being, existence), as we read above. To understand this concept even better, we may scrutinize the rest of the five substances through their ability to extend. They (the five substances other than the time) consist of an aggregate of units, they are in the form of *tiryaka-pracaya-skandha* (that which can extend in three dimensions is called *tiryaka-pracaya*) and extension becomes their natural attribute (ibid.: 125). For example, the *ākāśa* (space) is spread vertically, horizontally and diagonally with its infinite space points called *pradeśa*. In contrast, the medium of motion, the medium of rest, the soul and the matter are said to consist of innumerable space points. Considering time, we analyse that the past has already gone and cannot exist in the now, except in our memories, which are caused either by our attachment or aversion, and the future, by any means, cannot exist in the present.

> Thus, only *kāla* is without *pradeśa*, i.e. space points. Only the present moment of *kāla* has existence. The present moment (*samaya*) is a single unit and, therefore, cannot expand in three dimensions.
>
> — Ibid.: 125

This understanding is nothing but freedom. As Eckhart Tolle describes, "The present moment holds the key to liberation" (2001: 19). As it provides freedom from thought, and one is able to access the true essence of being.

This is the beauty as well as the mystery of time that the practical time (*vyavahāra kāla*) is not the one that causes change as it seems superficial in comparison to the transcendental time (*niścaya kāla*).

> Substances like *jīva*, *pudgala*, etc. undergo transmutation every moment, that is, their modes go on changing every moment; this is caused by transcendental time. In other words, transcendental time is the mode of *jīva* and *ajīva*. — Mahendra Kumar 2010: 125

Singularity and Eternality of Time

The reason for the inclusion of time in the group of substances is that it possesses the traits that are required in a substance. For example, just like the rest of the substances, time is eternal and also individual. Time is singular like space and the mediums of motion and rest. However, "it is separated from them by lacking space points. One unit of time (*samaya*) forms the present" (Schubring 2000: 128). Which means time does not have an extension in space. Indeed, given these statements, it is not easy to imagine the mystery and beauty of time.

The beauty of the secrets of the universe lies in their objectivity, which is unbiased and exists irrespective of an explorer, be it time, space or any other substance. Being humans, it is the elegance of our most developed brain which is highly rational and keeps us on our toes searching for and rediscovering those secrets.

> Newton considered both space and time as independent, objective realities, their existence being neither dependent upon the percipient nor the things sustained or related by them.
>
> — Mahendra Kumar 2010: 52

In terms of the evolution of our brains, humans started to look out for the secrets of the cosmos only when we could. However, this does not mean that those secrets have only begun to exist since then.

WHY HAS TIME BEEN CONSIDERED A SUBSTANCE?

Time is philosophical indeed; due to its five features, time has been put into the group of substances.

> They are *vartanā* (duration), *pariṇāma* (change), *kriyā* (action), *paratva* (priority) and *aparatva* (posteriority). — Ibid.: 126

The meaning of *vartanā* (duration) is "existence for a certain period" (ibid.). To elaborate further,

> the realization of the existence of the self by each substance, in each of its modes, in every passing unit of time, is *vartanā*.
>
> — Varni 2014b: 526

Pariṇāma (change) is,

> whenever any substance undergoes transmutation, we naturally get an indication of its time-duration of transmutation.
>
> — Mahendra Kumar 2010: 126

Hence, we notice that despite not having an extension in space, time has a different kind of extension, which can be noticed as it passes by. Any *kriyā* (action) "includes motion (*gati*), which means an orderly change of positions in space" (ibid.: 127). As we discussed earlier, as soon as we consider even one dimension of space, time inevitably gets added as a different dimension. Hence, when we say a substance is in motion, it means it is changing its position in space and, obviously, it is taking some time to do so. This is why any action is observable only through the space–time.

Paratva (priority) and *aparatva* (posteriority) are evident by their English meanings: "*Paratva* means antecedence (or precedence) and *aparatva* means succession" (ibid.). The sequence of events or their simultaneity is possible due to the concept of time. In these qualities of time, we can see that though time does not have physical existence (*asti*), it flows along with each change happening in a substance. It is not the cause, but merely a spectator. Hence, we notice that the existence of time is inevitably "a part of objective reality" (ibid.) as each substance is changing its modes incessantly and it is able to do so because of the presence of time.

We may also understand it better by knowing that even if we do not move in space or even if we do not perform any action through our thoughts, something still keeps passing by, and that is time. Varni describes, "it is the benevolence of the time substance that it originates an action" (2014a: 83), or we may put it this way, "each action or inaction originates and ends in time, and there is no other way".

Time Cycle in Jaina Philosophy

> *A cycle is hidden in each linear occurrence, just like a linear pattern is in each cyclic one.*

The theory of evolution takes an interesting twist when we see it through the lens of the time cycle. In Jaina philosophy, cosmic time is cyclic; hence, it neither has a beginning nor an end. It is divided into two *kāla*s mainly: *utsarpiṇī* and *avasarpiṇī*. Each of these is again subdivided into six time periods. Whereas *utsarpiṇī* refers to the increase of height, age, beauty, wealth, happiness, knowledge, wisdom and all the other positive traits, with the passing of time, *avasarpiṇī* is the opposite of that, i.e. all the mentioned traits decrease as the time passes. Currently, we are in the fifth era (*ārā*) of *avasarpiṇī kāla*. The duration of the first three time periods seems beyond our numerical understanding as they are described in years we cannot measure.

Even the fourth era is immeasurably long; however, the ancient Indian thinkers have described the length as the same as the number we get after subtracting 42,000 years from 1e + 14 (this is the number we get when we multiply 10 million by 10 million). The fifth and sixth *kāla*s are 21,000 years each; almost 2,700 years have passed since the current period, which is the fifth era (*duṣamā kāla* or *pañcama kāla*). After this period, *duṣamā-duṣamā kāla* of the same length will come, which will be a time of extreme grief. Abstract translated from the *Jainendra Siddhānta Kośa* puts humans in *duṣamā-duṣamā kāla* as mentioned in the text *Tiloyapaṇṇatti*[32] as under:

---

[32] *mūlapaphala-macchādi, savvāṇaṁ māṇusāṇa āhāro tāhe vāsā vacchā, geha-ppahudī ṇarā ṇa dīsaṁti* । — 1558

tatto ṇaggā savve, bhavaṇa-vihīṇā vaṇesu hiṇḍaṁtā savvaṅga-dhūma- →

Body: The height at entering this time period is three or three and a half hands (i.e. 3-4 ft approximately).

Appearance: Their appearance resembles apes and their bodies smell bad.

Age: The maximum age span is 20 years.

Residence: They do not have houses; they are homeless and wander naked in the forests. There are no trees, nor do they have livestock.

Physiological miseries: Often, the demeanour of humans is beastly, ruthless, deaf, blind, dumb, impoverished and short-tempered. Their bodies are filled with diseases. They do not have families.

As time passes, their height, age and strength keep decreasing.

(Please note that due to the difference between the author and publisher, the *gāthā* numbers have been changed in the *Jainendra Siddhānta Kośa* as *gāthā* 1535 to 1542 (Varni 2014: 90) also, the chapter has been mentioned as chapter 4.)

← *vaṇṇā, go dhamma-parāyaṇā kūrā* । — 1559

bahirā aṅdhā kāṇā, mūkā dāridda-kūḍa-paripuññā dīṇā vāṇara-rūvā, aimecchā huṇḍasaṁthāṇā । — 1560

kujjā vāmaṇa-taṇuṇo, ṇāṇāviha-vāhi-veyaṇā-viyalā bahu-koha-loha-mohā, paurāhārā sahāva-pāviṭṭhā । — 1561

saṁbaddha-sajaṇa-baṁdhava-dhaṇa-putta-kalatta-mitta-parihīṇā phuḍīdaṁga-phuḍīda-kesā, jūvā-likkhāhī saṁ-chaṇṇā । — 1562

— Vrishabhacharya 2006: 448

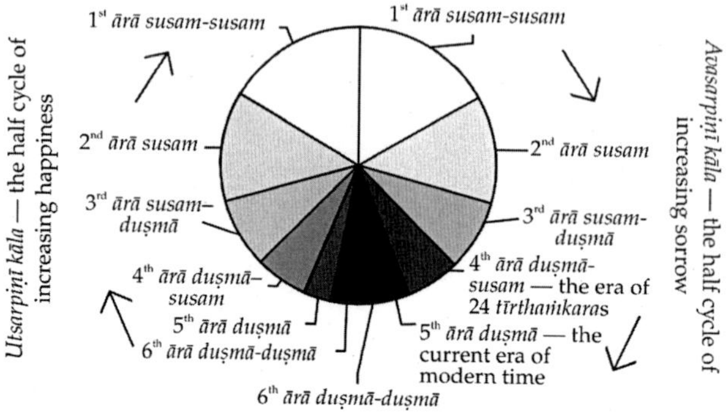

Source: "Jain Cosmology". Web. 15th October, 2019. <en.wikipedia.org/wiki/Jain_cosmology>

fig. 2.1: The Jaina cosmic wheel of time

To compare the collective situation of the human race from the last time period of the descending cycle, which is of extreme misery, and from the last time period of the ascending cycle, which is of extreme happiness, let us now have a glimpse of the description of humans given in the text *Tiloyapaṇṇatti*[33] upon entering the sixth time period of the *utsarpiṇī kāla* (the half cycle of increasing happiness):

Body: The height of the humans at entering this time period is 2 *kosas* (1 *kosa* is equal to 1.8 km).

Appearance: Their complexion is that of a full moon and they have 128 bones in their spine.

---

33 *do kosā uccheho, ṇāri-ṇarā puṇṇamindu-sarisa-muhā bahuviṇaya-sīlavaṁtā, biguṇīya-causaṭṭhī-puṭṭhī* — 1623

susamasusamābhiṣāṇo, tāhe pavisedi chaṭṭhamo kālo tassa paḍhame paese, āū — pahudīṇī puvvaṁ va 1624 *kāla-sahāva-baleṇaṁ, vaḍḍhante tāi maṇuva — tiriyāṇaṁ tāhe esa dharitti, uttamabhogāvaṇī tti supasiddho* — 1625

— Shri Yati Vrishabhacharya 2006: 464

Age: Their age is 2 *palyas* (*palya* is the unit given by the Jaina thinkers to measure the immeasurable time).

Demeanour: They are extremely humble and virtuous. Their bodies are free of diseases. As time passes, their height, age, beauty and the availability of the natural resources on the earth keep increasing.

The clock, the calendar, the seasons, and movements of the sun, the moon and planets are all cyclic. It is the soul substance that keeps evolving and devolving amongst these. It keeps going through the cycles in countless physical manifestations, generating causes and, in turn, enduring their effects, curating its destiny. Until one day it realizes that it has the inevitable, innate ability to know how the cycles take place and in knowing so, the soul realizes that it is not the cycles that will end, but it is itself that has to be withdrawn from these.

After analysing evolution by considering the time cycle, we see that neither evolution is permanent nor devolution and that devolution eventually leads to evolution. According to the time cycle in Jaina philosophy, the next *utsarpiṇī kāla* (the half cycle of increasing happiness) will start with the sixth time zone, i.e. *duṣamā-duṣamā kāla* (time of extreme grief), it will proceed towards *duṣmā kāla* (time similar to the current times) and, eventually, till the first time period which is *suṣamā-suṣamā kāla* (time of extreme happiness). The mere thought of attaining a state of the most spiritually evolved beings is calming, as if we have found a base for our existence.

Ancient Indian wisdom indicates that we are but individuals travelling collectively on our respective journeys. We can influence others around us and, in turn, can get influenced by them. However, during this interchange of ideas and energies, we do not lose the essence of our individual journeys. And that the time cycle is never-ending, the matter, being a non-living entity, cannot have a quest; however, as conscious beings, we can wilfully choose to withdraw ourselves from this cycle.

Cosmology

Irrespective of our birthplace or the community we are born in, we keep hearing the concepts of heavens and hells since childhood. Where a wrongdoer sows the seeds of a terrible destiny that is bound to take him into the fires of hell and the one who chooses to lead an ethical life binds good *karma* that causes future births in the heavens. We all wonder if these places truly exist. However, under the compulsion of being rational thinkers, we dismiss the existence of similar dimensions, as they cannot be accessed by logical means. Well, the dimensions of heavens and hells are indeed mentioned in our ancient texts. They may also be called upward and downward dimensions respectively.

Despite this belief that we endure what we have done here and now, on this planet, and in this life, countless examples motivate us to contemplate the presence of such expansions somewhere in the universe. They can be called different universes, planets, lands or dimensions, and there can be different modes to travel there, unknown to mankind. These dimensions may not be known through the mind, as the modern spiritual teacher Eckhart Tolle (2001: 45) writes:

> The mind cannot know. It can only know facts or information, through labels, judgements, and opinions about a specific thing.

What about that which cannot be known through rationale but can only be experienced and realized deep within? The ancient texts of timeless wisdom need our attention, especially when we know that this wisdom is being expressed by no one but the people who perceived the absolute truth.

Jaina philosophy analyses every aspect of truth through different points of view. In the context of understanding the universe, there are four points of view to enquire,

> (i) from substance-point of view, (ii) from space-point of view, (iii) from time-point of view, and (iv) from modes-point of view.
>
> — Mahendra Kumar 2010: 131

The universe is made up of *pañcāstikāya* (five existents). Despite having its own individual entity, each of them lives together with the rest unitedly in a certain space known as cosmic space. Hence, from the point of view of substances, "the universe is a unitary entity" (Ibid.: 168). From the point of view of space, "the universe has an end" (ibid.). As we studied earlier also, the cosmic space (*lokākāśa*) is finite.

From the perspective of time,

> the universe was never non-existent; it is never non-existent; it will never be non-existent; it was, it is, and it will always be. It is eternal, fixed, perennial, indestructible, imperishable, and ever-present, thus infinite. — Mahendra Kumar 2010: 168

The unique way of multiple point of views to scrutinize the aspects of reality is not only beautiful and mysterious but it also provides immense scope for further research about the magnificence of the same.

A substance keeps changing and modifying its attributes continuously.

> The degree of the attributes (of a given object) with each passing unit of time is its mode (*paryāya*). — Varni 2014b: 45

Hence, each substance has countless modes present in it parallelly, and some of them may be contradictory to each other. For example, an apple has a sweet fragrance of its taste at the time of being edible. But the same apple changes its fragrance as soon as it starts to rot. It also keeps changing its colours as well. Hence, the same apple has one mode of appearing healthy and the other mode of rotting.

Similarly, each object in "the world has infinite modes of colours, an infinite number of smell-modes, an infinite number of taste-modes" (Mahendra Kumar 2010: 169). Modes keep changing persistently. Hence, through the point of view of modes, the universe is infinite as each substance in it passes through one or more of its infinite modes at any given time.

Universe in Jaina Philosophy

The shape of the universe (*loka* or the cosmos) in Jaina philosophy is very distinct.

> *Lokākāśa* is schematically depicted as a hexagon resting on an inverted conical section with a flat base having a finite thickness. .Various parts, from top down, are called *siddha śilā* (space of purity), stated to be the abode of *siddhas*, *ūrdhvaloka* (heaven, abode of *devas*), *madhya loka* (abode of humans, animals and other living beings) and *adholoka* (abode of hellish beings). Each are subdivided into seven distinct regions. In addition, there is *trasanāḍī* connecting the top of *loka* to the bottom, half way along the depth of *loka*.
>
> — Bhandari 2015: 139

Trasanāḍī depicts that all life forms, be it heavenly or hellish beings, or humans, animals, plants, birds and the rest, reside in the limited boundary of it, which is located at the exact centre of the cosmos. To understand these three dimensions, better, we may call the *ūrdhva-loka*, the upward vertical dimension, and *adholoka*, the downward vertical dimension, and the middle region (*madhya loka*) can be called the horizontal dimension.

The ancient philosophers from India used to explain objects, things, ideas, etc. with reference to one's surroundings. In the context of the shape of the universe, the Jaina thinkers explained the same:

> With reference to the human body and conceived the idea of *Loka Puruṣa*. It is compared to a *puruṣa* (human). Each part, be it the upper, the middle or the lower, is the object of meditation. Mahāvīra used to meditate upon all three of them.
>
> — Mahaprajna 2013: 112

The human body can easily be divided into three parts by anyone who contemplates: the upper, the middle and the lower. The upper part of the human body contains the following:

1. The brain is located at the topmost part of the body and can be compared to a computer's Central Processing Unit (CPU).

It is the root of human intelligence and makes us the most rational beings on the planet.

2. All the five senses of touch, sight, smell, hearing and taste, out of which, the skin pervades the whole body.
3. The mind is an abstract concept and can be defined as "the part of the person that makes it possible for him to think, feel emotions and understand things",[34] and that which enables one to decide between right and wrong or, in other words, that which plays the role of the conscience.
4. The heart, despite possessing the quality of pumping clean blood with the help of the lungs throughout the body, has some abstract tasks, too. For example, the heart feels hurt whenever one is heavy with emotions.

The middle part consists majorly of the digestive system, due to which one keeps bound to earn a living. The body's lower part possesses the reproductive and excretory organs, which represent the downward vertical dimensions.

When one keenly observes the map of the universe and tries to relate it to one's own body by asking the question: Why is our body the way it is? Why and how are humans the best species on the planet? One speculates the following answers: the shape and structure of our body represent the shape of the universe. Being the best-developed species, each human represents an individual universe in himself and the lower part (the part below the belly where reproductive and excretory organs are located) represents the *adholoka*. The middle part (of the body), i.e. stomach, kidneys, liver, lungs, etc., represents the *madhya loka*, because of which all wander into the infinite cycles of birth and death; all these organs are related to the most basic necessities of a living being, which is

---

34 "Mind", Cambridge Dictionary, 2021, <https://dictionary.cambridge.org/dictionary/english/mind> (accessed on 3 October 2021).

hunger, which keeps one on a spree to earn bread and so on and so forth. The belly button is the exact centre of our body, through which each of us is connected to our mothers, who brought us into this world and through which we bind ourselves in different emotions and relationships. Being the exact centre of our body, the belly button represents the Meru, which is the exact centre of the universe as depicted in all Indian philosophies.

The upper part, i.e. the location of the five senses, the heart, and the mind, represents the *ūrdhvaloka*. Considering precisely the uppermost part of the brain, it represents the *siddha śilā* (abode of the liberated souls). As we now know the top centre of the brain is called the crown *cakra* (*sahasrāra cakra*).

The crown *cakra* is the centre of spiritual consciousness and divine oneness. It is also the centre of self-realization.[35]

Perhaps this is why the brain is located in the topmost realm of the human body, for it can know and achieve the absolute in the cosmos.

Narendra Bhandari[36] in his book *Jainism: The Eternal and Universal Path to Enlightenment* speculates:

> Some current theories, like the string theory, suggest that the universe may have eleven dimensions, ten of space and one of time, instead of the four-dimension space–time universe. It is difficult to draw a multidimensional object on a two-dimensional paper. The sketch of *lokākāśa* in the image given may be a projection of a four (or eleven) dimensional object on a two-dimensional sheet of paper. — 2015: 140

---

35 Master Choa Kok Sui, The Chakras and Their Functions:The Crown Chakra/Sahasrara Chakra and Your Will Power, Worldpranichealing.com, <https://www.worldpranichealing.com/en/chakra/sahasrara/> (accessed on 5 October 2021).

36 More information about Narendra Bhandari at www.nbhandari.com.

Modern Cosmology

The famous scientist Fred Hoyle (1915 – 2001[37]), who rejected the Big Bang Theory, gave a broader definition of the universe:

> The Universe is everything, both living and inanimate things, both atoms and galaxies and if the spiritual exists as well as the material, of spiritual things also; and if there is a Heaven and a Hell, of Heaven and Hell too; for by its very nature the Universe is the totality of all things. — 1955: 304

As soon as one starts to get convinced about a metaphysical topic it takes one to the voyage of the different subtopics of that topic and, eventually, one finds that each of them is interrelated. As Hoyle mentioned, there are two dimensions of each concept: one is the material and the other is the abstract. He also emphasized that the physical and spiritual worlds exist in the same universe, as the universe is the whole of every concept, subject, living being, matter, etc.

Considering the eleven dimensions of the universe as speculated by Narendra Bhandari and keeping in mind how Hoyle described the totality of the universe, we may take the map of the universe, as described in the ancient texts of Jaina philosophy, as symbolic. Bhandari (2015: 139-40) says:

> *The Diagram* (*fig.* 2.2) does not represent the actual geometry or structure of the universe but symbolically represents some other features of the universe.

Here, we must keep in mind that if we consider the section marked by *T* (*trasanāḍī*) in *fig.* 2.2 as the worm hole that connects different parts of the universe, even this worm hole exists in the finite boundaries of the cosmic space known as *lokākāśa* in Jainism.

> The physical universe is made of six components: space, time, matter (and energy), and three forces (gravitation, electroweak and strong nuclear forces). Whereas, Jainism states the material

[37] Fred Hoyle, Wikipedia, 28 September 2021, <https://en.wikipedia.org/wiki/Fred_Hoyle> (accessed on 8 October 2021).

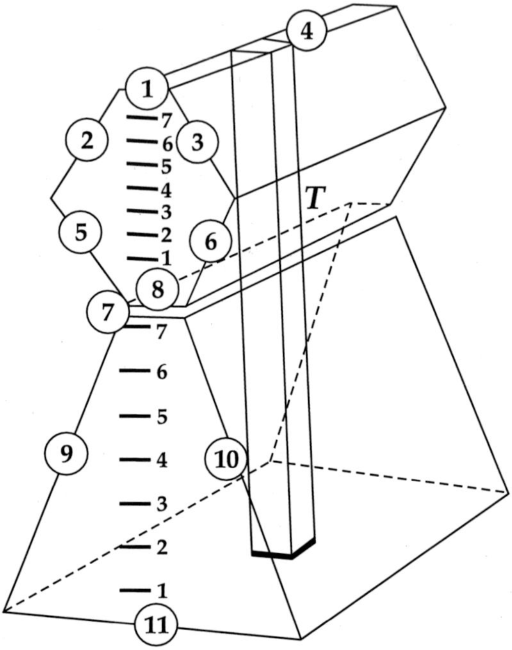

Explanation: Jaina *lokākāśa* showing its eleven arms, as marked. Each arm may symbolically represent a dimensional universe, with the string theory (*M*-theory) which envisages an eleven-dimensional universe, with ten dimensions of space and the eleventh dimension, marked by 4, representing time. The *trasanāḍī* (*T*) is proposed to be a worm hole that connects various parts of the universe.

fig. 2.2: Structure of the universe according to Jaina scriptures

> universe is composed of five components: space, time, matter, *dharmāstikāya* and *adharmāstikāya*. — Bhandari 2015: 97

Indian philosophy considers the three forces to be material only. Hence, we notice the accordance between modern cosmology and Jaina philosophy on at least three essentials of the universe: space, time and matter. However, the existence of the other two constituents — medium of motion and medium of rest, *dharmāstikāya* and *adharmāstikāya*, respectively — has yet to be proven by experiments.

Interestingly, Indian philosophies also mention the unique and perhaps the most essential element that contributes to the possibility of the universe's existence: the *jīva dravya* (soul substance). This is the only spiritual component, and its study seems to be the most worthwhile to introduce one to the rest of the abstract dimensions of the universe. Without this, all these studies, experiments and discoveries would not have been possible in the first place.

Discovered in 1925[38] by a group of scientists, the most recent branch of sciences is quantum mechanics, which puts harsh limitations on the level of certainty of our knowledge. Besides particle–wave duality,

> the concept in quantum mechanics is that every particle or quantum entity may be described as either a particle or a wave.[39]

Another precept of this branch of science is that

> the universe does not exist if you do not observe it. This implies that the universe and the observer exist together as a pair and neither can exist without the other. — Bhandari 2015: 101

The existence of any object is useless if there is no (conscious) entity to observe it.

When we meekly try to analyse the mind-boggling vastness of the universe, we realize that we are smaller even than a sand particle searching for the secrets of the universe with its minimal resources. Michio Kaku writes:

> It may seem eerie that we humans are able to talk so glibly about

---

[38] History of Quantum Mechanics, Wikipedia.org, 30 September 2021, <https://en.wikipedia.org/wiki/History_of_quantum_mechanics> (accessed on 14 October 2021).

[39] Wave Particle Duality, Wikipedia.org, 13 October 2021, <https://en.wikipedia.org/wiki/Wave%-E2%80%93particle_duality> (accessed on 15 October 2021).

> temperatures and events so cataclysmic that they would rip apart our earth (even our galaxy). — Kaku and Thompson 1995: 133

Physicist Steven Weinberg writes in his book *The First Three Minutes: A Modern View of the Origin of the Universe*:

> I cannot deny the feeling of unreality in writing about the first three minutes as if we really know what we are talking about.[40]

Whatever we imagine or observe can only be possible because it exists somewhere in the universe, be it a dream, a thought or a realization. No one knows if an artist's creation, an author's pen or a dreamer's dream takes one to which dimensions of the universe through their imaginations, as "even our imaginations are too conservative" (Kaku and Thompson 1995: 200).

There are mainly two aspects of reality: one that can be seen and observed directly through the senses and mind, and the other philosophical, which probes further and tries to find the reason for the existence of any given object, situation, personality, etc. in all its possibilities, with all its dimensions. These aspects are two sides of the same coin: one is materialist and the other is spiritual. Both express different elements of truth.

> It is as much as light can exhibit the properties of either particles or waves, depending on the way in which it is considered, but it is something more than either of these: it is light!
>
> — Mardia and Rankin 2013: 81

If humankind starts to respect spirituality as much as it values material science, countless gateways of knowledge will be opened and accessible.

Metaphysics

When I say I belong to this world, does that mean "that" world also exists?

---

40 Steven Weinberg, Noosphe.re, 25 July 2020, <https://www.noosphe.re/post/624640868047093760/i-cannot-deny-a-feeling-of-unreality-in-writing> (accessed on 16 October 2021).

Metaphysics is a complicated subject that is hard to define. However, there are many descriptions available; according to the *Merriam-Webster Dictionary*, metaphysics is

> a division of philosophy that is concerned with the fundamental nature of reality and being.[41]

Another definition is:

> It is a branch of philosophy that studies the first principles of being, identity and change, space and time, causality, necessity and possibility:[42]

In the pursuit of knowledge, one realizes that not only philosophers and thinkers but even common people have metaphysical queries. For example, when we talk about space and time, one need not be a student of physics. Travelling from one place to another is also called space travel, as we are crossing innumerable space units to reach that place. Getting the gist of the present moment can be considered understanding time.

> When we speak of the object of (metaphysical) experience, we refer to it as reality (or ultimate real) or as "being", "what is", "what truly exists". — Mahendra Kumar 2010: 14

Pondering metaphysics, we eventually conclude that a conscious entity observes and seeks reality. After all the research, the conscious entity finds itself to be that metaphysical entity. When it tries to know the absolute reality, it starts to discriminate between the physical world and its own pure, unaltered entityhood. However, easier said than done, it is not an easy process.

Cambridge Dictionary of Philosophy elaborates on metaphysics:

---

41 "Metaphysics", Merriam-Webster.com, <https://www.merriam-webster.com/dictionary/metaphysics> (accessed on 20 October 2021).

42 "Metaphysics", Wikipedia.org, 18 October 2021, <https://en.wikipedia.org/wiki/Metaphysics> (accessed on 20 October 2021).

> On account of knowledge, our knowledge of the world is extremely limited, concerning both its spatial and temporal dimensions and its inner constitution, we must allow for an indefinite number of possible ways the world may be, might have been, or will be. — Audi 2017: 662

Despite the continuous changes in a specific object, something underneath remains intact and its primary reality remains unchanged. Metaphysics is to know that unchanged constant beneath the constant changes.

Aristotle describes in his work *Metaphysics*:

> Each entity must have the most general and necessary characteristics in order to be counted as being. And those criteria are — every entity must be either an individual thing, or a property, or a relation, or an event, or a state of affairs, or a set.
> — AUDI

For example, the reader of this book and this book itself are two individual entities. Both have a few properties, such as the reader might wear glasses and the book has a certain shape. At present, the reader and the book share a relationship. There are plenty of events in the reader's life, like marriage, bearing children, etc. The reader goes through some or the other state of affairs incessantly, like travelling to work, eating out, etc. All readers around the world make a set of readers.

Now, we will study how the thinkers of the Indian philosophy of Jainism have described metaphysics.

Metaphysics in Jaina Philosophy

In the philosophy of Jainism, there are not only various definitions of an existent but also different categories of truth, which solve our metaphysical queries efficiently. Ācārya Umāsvāti mentions in his treatise on the nature of reality, *Tattvārthasūtra*,[43] "existence is the character of a substance" (Tatia 2011: 135). The foremost requirement for enquiring further about any substance is its existence. This existence can be physical (as in the case of matter) or abstract (as in the case of consciousness). If there is an existence, it surely has some attributes and would be changing modes. Needless to say, those attributes and modes will inevitably be included in the existence of that specific substance. Ācārya Umāsvāti clarifies[44] further that "origination, cessation and persistence constitute existence" (Tatia 2011: 135). This teaching depicts that each existent is entering into a new mode with each passing unit of time, leaving its old mode behind. During this change in mode, its existence is intact.

According to Jaina philosophy, during the change in any substance, only the mode changes, and no matter what its substancehood remains the same. Hence, with each passing unit of time, everything (be it living or non-living) is changing; during a specific change, a new mode comes into existence (*utpāda*) and the old one gets destroyed (*vyaya*); during these incessant changes, the essence of that substance stays the same. Here, the continuity amongst all modes is persistence (*dhrauvya*).

The trio of origination, cessation and persistence can also be looked upon through the perspective of qualities and modes. Another definition of substance given in the *Tattvārthasūtra*[45] is, "that which possesses qualities and modes is a substance" (Tatia 2011: 142). The degree of attributes and the modes are temporary and vary continuously. However, the one who possesses these degrees and modes is the unchanged substance in the real sense. For example, gold is the same substance as gold when it is in the raw

---

43 *ṣaḍ dravyalakṣaṇaṁ* । — *Tattvārthasūtra* 5.29

44 *utpāda-vyaya-dhrauvyayuktaṁ sat* । — *Tattvārthasūtra* 5.30

45 *guṇa-paryāyavad dravyam* । — 5.37

form mixed with the rocks and soil in the mines. It is the same when taken out from the mines and moulded into a piece of jewellery. It is the same substance during all the changes in its modes, from a bangle to a coin to a necklace and so on. Where being able to conduct heat and electricity is its innate quality. Despite being mixed with other metals to convert it into white or rose gold, it does not leave its essence of being gold. Similarly, in the context of consciousness, the Indian thinkers convey that the soul always remains the soul, irrespective of its immemorial association with matter, in the form of different *karmas*. It is never bereft of its innate attributes of knowledge and perception.

Categories of truth as described in the text on reality: Tattvārtha Sūtra

> Reality is absolute and can only be realized. To describe it, we need relativity; for that, we need language, symbols and labels.

No matter how underdeveloped it is, each living being desires freedom. However, being the most developed species, we are the ones who can aim for absolute freedom through the right knowledge. This may be a concrete question: as humans, why do we always look forward to knowing? The answer ancient texts provide is — because our true nature is to know and to perceive. In that sense, knowledge is freedom. Apart from worldly affairs, when one seeks truth, one aims to become fearless, calm, compassionate and enlightened by the knowledge one gains. In this context, enquiry into the categories of truth contributes immensely to getting the seeker on the right path.

Ācārya Umāsvāti wrote the text on reality, *Tattvārthasūtra*, to solve these dilemmas. He describes not only the categories of truth but also the rules for counting those categories as ones. These rules are rational and philosophical, motivating the seeker to contemplate them profoundly.

In the very first chapter of the text, Umāsvāti describes that there are seven categories of truth:[46]

> (1) souls (sentient entities or *jīva*), (2) non-sentient entities (*ajīva*), (3) the inflow of kārmic particles to the soul (*āsrava*), (4) binding of the kārmic particles to the soul (*bandha*), (5) stopping the inflow of kārmic particles (*saṁvara*), (6) the falling away of kārmic particles (*nirjarā*), (7) liberation from worldly (kārmic) bondage (*mokṣa*).
>
> — Tatia 2011: 6

When we discuss the eternal nature of the substances that create this visible and abstract universe, we come to know that not only the non-sentient substance (or non-living matter) but also the sentient substance (or the consciousness) are indestructible and, hence, eternal. Also, despite being opposite, interestingly, they fulfil the rules to be counted in the categories of truth. The observable and unobservable cosmos is an incessant interaction of these two substances. Hence, there are mainly these two categories and the rest of the five are different forms of non-living matter only.

Further, there are ways to analyse these categories by different means. In another *sūtra*, Ācārya Umāsvāti mentions:[47]

> The categories of truth and the enlightened world view, etc., can be analysed by name, symbol, potentiality and actuality.
>
> — Ibid.: 7

For example, we give a name to an object made up of non-living matter (e.g. this is a table; that is a computer) and also to the manifestation of the consciousness in the form of a being (e.g. that is an ant; I am a human, and we also give a specific name to different beings). We designate symbols to indicate an idea, a concept or an object. Inevitably, a symbol can only be given to something that falls under the category of truth. For example, humans have invented

---

[46] *jīvā-jīvāsrava-bandha-saṁvara-nirjarā-mokṣās tattvam* ।
— *Tattvārthasūtra* 1.4

[47] *nāma-sthāpanā-dravya-bhāvatas tannyāsaḥ* । — *Tattvārthasūtra* 1.5

alphabets, different sets of alphabets form words that eventually help us to express our feelings, emotions, etc., and also to know reality through philosophical queries and scientific experiments.

Also, each object has the potential to be moulded into a certain shape due to the presence of countless absolute atoms at its base. Similarly, each consciousness has the potential to manifest itself in different bodies according to the actions it performs. Needless to clarify, the actuality of the non-living matter and the consciousness, as we see, observe and realize both around us at all times.

Further, Ācārya Umāsvāti clarifies:[48]

> The categories can be understood with great accuracy through the approved means of knowledge and the philosophical standpoints.
> — Tatia 2011: 8

Mainly,

> the approved means of knowledge are twofold: immediate (innate) and mediate (acquired).
> — Tatia 2011: 8.

They can also be understood as direct (*pratyakṣa*) and indirect (*apratyakṣa*) knowledge, respectively. Direct knowledge is that which we gain directly, without any medium of senses and the mind, such as self-realization. Indirect knowledge is gained through mediums; for example, students go to school or college to gain knowledge through books, websites, etc. Whichever knowledge we gain in our lives falls under the category of indirect knowledge.

Depending upon the student's intellect, one aspect of reality can only be understood at a time, that too, using one specific philosophical standpoint. However, with time, experience and dedication, the student becomes more efficient and able to grasp many aspects of truth at once.

A philosophical standpoint takes the student of reality to a deeper understanding of the nature of things. However, being a mode of indirect knowledge,

---

48 *pramāṇa-nayair-adhigamaḥ* । — *Tattvārthasūtra* 1.6

> philosophical standpoint gives a limited view of what is presented in its unlimited character by the approved means of knowledge.
>
> — Ibid.

Despite their limitations, philosophical standpoints take the seeker closer to the truth.

Ācārya Umāsvāti leaves no stone unturned in describing the categories of truth in detail:[49]

> The categories (and their attributes) are understood in detail in terms of definition, possession, cause, location, duration and varieties. — Tatia 2011: 8.

The categories of truth, i.e. the consciousness and the non-living matter, further accomplish these subcategories. Both of them can be defined, possess specific attributes, are the causes of the existence of the universe, have a certain location at all times at some space point of the cosmos, and their modes have a duration. Lastly, there are varieties of both of them. For example, consciousness is defined as one with knowledge and perception as its inseparable, eternal traits. It possesses infinite bliss and power, and can cause change in the non-living matter. In the context of location, it is located in any one of the dimensions of the habitable universe at any given time. In terms of duration, it is eternal; however, its modes keep changing. When it comes to varieties, despite all souls being equal, they appear diverse because they are situated on different steps on the ladder of evolution.

The quest to know the categories of truth does not end here when the saint describes:[50]

> To explore further the categories of truth and the enlightened world view, there are the gateways of existence, numerical

[49] *nirdeśa-svāmitva-sādhanādhikaraṇa-sthiti-vidhānataḥ* ।
— *Tattvārthasūtra* 1.7

[50] *sat-saṁkhyā-kṣetra-sparśana-kālāṁtara-bhāvalpabahutveś ca* ।
— *Tattvārthasūtra* 1.8

determination, field occupied, field touched, continuity, time-lapse, states and relative numerical strength. — Tatia 2011: 9

The journey of life is to peel off the layers of ignorance and try to get closer to what is real. When one owns the kind of view, which sees beyond the surface existence, it is known as the enlightened world view. Knowing and analysing the categories of truth initiates the process of freedom from thought and eventually from the cycle of cause and effect.

To know and understand the categories of truth and even the tiniest things, we need numbers and ways to measure the specifics of the given object, which lead to the gateway of numerical determination. Be it conscious or non-living, each category occupies some space in each of its manifestations; this way, both occupy a certain part of the field and also touch the same. Despite continuously changing modes, each category has continuity in its existence. Both categories can be observed through time-lapse to see their different modes. Both have certain states through relative and absolute perspectives. Lastly, as consciousness and matter are both subject to relativity, each has relative numerical strength that can be compared with fellow souls or matter for different purposes.

There is ample scope for further research to analyse the gateways of the categories of truth.

Metaphysics of Paramāṇu (Absolute Atom)

Ācārya Kundakunda describes the absolute part of non-living matter in the text about the five substances that constitute the whole universe, *pañcāstikāya*[51] (the word means five substances) that have existence (*asti*) and quality of extension in space (*kāya*) as:

A *paramāṇu*, consists of only one *pradeśa* (i.e. one space point), is the terminus of the divisibility of matter, is by itself without

[51] *sarveṣāṁ skandhānāṁ yoantyastāṁ vijānīhi paramāṇu* ।
sa śāśvatoaśabdaḥ ekoavibhāgī mūrtibhavaḥ ॥ — *Pañcāstikāya* 3.77

> beginning, end, or middle, is destitute of sound, and is coupled with the qualities of taste, touch, smell, and colour.
>
> — Sogani 2001: 25

It is interesting to know that when we talk about the smallest indivisible part of matter and that it occupies the smallest indivisible part of space, the abstract reality of time inevitably enters the scenario as the third substance. The smallest indivisible unit of time, known as *samaya* in Jaina philosophy, is the time taken to measure the smallest part of matter into space; it is also called *niścaya kāla* (transcendental time). This way, when we inquire about an object in the deepest manner, we get three substances: one is matter, the second is space and the third is time. Hence, the space–time duo can be converted into a trio by adding matter and it can be called space–time–matter.

Further Ācārya Kundakunda describes:[52]

> That which is described as corporeal and is the cause of the four elements — earth, water, fire and air — is to be known as the absolute atom (*paramāṇu*). It has the quality of modification and, by itself, is without sound. —Jain 2020: 153

The non-living matter (*pudgala*) is tangible. However, despite being the foundation of each object, the absolute atom can never be seen by any means and can only be observed and touched in groups. Like any other substance, the modes of the absolute atom also keep changing.

Ācārya Kundakunda clarifies further:[53]

> Again, it is devoid of sound, but is the cause of sound, i.e. the

---

52 *ādeśamātramūrttaḥ dhātucatuṣkasya kāraṇaṁ vastu* ।
sa jñeyaḥ paramāṇuḥ pariṇāmaguṇaḥ svayamaśabdaḥ ॥
— *Pañcāstikāya* 3.78

53 *śabdaḥ skandhaprabhavaḥ skandhaḥ paramāṇu saṁgasaṁghātaḥ* ।
spr̥ṣṭeṣu teṣu jāyate śabda utpādako niyataḥ ॥ — Ibid. 3.79

> combination of atoms may produce sound when they strike against other aggregates of atoms.[54]

The *paramāṇu* itself is destitute of sound, but is the creator of sound when in action with its similar counterparts. The efforts of a single being in a specific direction do not create a stir, whereas similar efforts by a group not only get noticed but also bring results. Metaphysics appears to be the science of illusion; however, it clearly is not.

Further attributes of the absolute atom are:[55]

> It is indestructible and eternal, is responsible for the disruption of *skandhas* (groups) by virtue of its segregation from them, is also the substantial cause of them and can be used as the measure of time (*samaya*). — Sogani 2001: 25

Like the rest of the substances, even the *paramāṇu* can neither be destroyed by any means nor have a beginning or end. Just like a single person can start the disintegration of a humongous organization by stepping out of its initiatives, the absolute atom causes the disintegration of a group of its similar equivalents. The absolute atom is used to measure absolute time and absolute space.

Metaphysics, Ethics, Cause and Effect

Analysing the workings of the cosmos by breaking down its building blocks takes us on a beautiful metaphysical journey. At this point, the researcher starts to ponder whether a metaphysical relationship exists between our thoughts, how we live, our actions and the cosmos. The philosophy of Jainism provides an affirmative answer to this query. Zydenbos writes:

> Morality, psychology, good health, metaphysics and many other .matters are all aspects of human life and are interlinked.
>
> — 2006: 21

---

54 English tr. of *Pañcāstikāya*, *sūtra* 79 from *EDJ*, pp. 25-26.

55 *nityo nānavakāśo na sāvakāśaḥ pradeśato bhettā* ।
skandhānāmapi ca karttā pravibhaktā kālasaṁkhyāyāḥ ॥
— *Pañcāstikāya* 3.80

This way, even one's morality falls under the ambit of metaphysics, where the universe inevitably works as the mediator to serve one whatever one has sown for oneself. With each of one's actions, one is incessantly creating causes that are inevitably getting stored (in the form of tiny kārmic matter) into the space points of the universe, effects of which are inevitably to be served back to that specific person only, who created the cause at the first place. According to Indian philosophy, this is but the law of nature. Zydenbos states further:

> Jainism can be considered a kind of system of laws, but they are considered natural rather than moral. — Ibid.: 20

This way, the Jainas do not have a rule book, written by a higher being, to be followed strictly to attain salvation. Each being is free to create a cause, the effect of which would be endured by that being only as the inevitable universal law. That being is also free to analyse the cycle of cause and effect, as per its own intellect, by self-experience, studying under the guidance of a teacher or by any other means. Eventually, it can step ahead onto the ladder of self-growth. For example, if someone has a lost temper, even at the slightest adversity, he gets angry and starts creating chaos for the people around him. However, with age, he realizes through self-experience that his anger has done much harm to him and his relationships, whereas if he could have controlled the same, his life would have been much easier and healthier. Hence, at a certain point, he transforms and becomes calm. In this example, we see that the person was not told by someone to control his anger. He realized the harm of the same on his own. In the same way, anyone, irrespective of their geographical location, the community they are born into and the surrounding circumstances, can proceed on the spiritual path of their free will. Such is the accessibility and universality of the metaphysical laws of the cosmos.

When one tries to find meaning in one's life, one tries to connect the dots between each happening and persona. Eventually, one concludes that the relation between cause and effect is objective and rational. One inevitably becomes a metaphysicist and analyses everything through the sieve of this subject, finding that everything matters, be it one's actions, reactions, thoughts, eating habits, relationships, as profession. When contemplating on cause and effect, questions like these may bother one: "Why am I here at this particular moment? What is the purpose of life? Why did this certain incident happen with me only?", etc. At this specific time, the *karma* theory comes into the scene to provide solace, which is actually the detailed study of cause and effect.

Direct realization of the universality of cause and effect can lead to further contemplation on the cause of one's birth, the effect of which is death. Then comes the query: What caused one's birth? Hence,

> metempsychosis, as a rule, is combined with the acceptance of the doctrine of *karma*, which is essentially an extension of the principle of cause and effect into the metaphysical realm.
>
> — Zydenbos 2006: 56

And then the being is bound to have the following philosophical query,

> just as I can harm my health in this life by certain unwise actions, I can harm the quality of my next life by certain other actions.
>
> — Ibid.

Through this perspective, the being starts to be at peace with life and begins to deal the adversity with wisdom. Eventually, such contemplation leads the person to react with less intensity, which in turn creates fewer effects for the future. This way, the being starts to climb up the ladder of consciousness evolution. Hence, we see how metaphysics is linked with ethics.

Metaphysics, Knowledge and Perception

It may be an interesting question: Why do we always want to know? What does it serve us? Well, according to Indian philosophy, the nature of consciousness is to know and to perceive. This way, the more one knows, the clearer one's perception becomes. One starts to see the pattern in the bigger picture of life. This journey of gaining knowledge and enhancing perception is freeing, for it takes one to one's true nature. Ācārya Umāsvāti writes in *Tattvārthasūtra*,[56] the text on the nature of reality, "sentience is the defining characteristic of the soul" (Tatia 2011: 39).

> *Upayoga* is the distinctive, innate accomplishment of consciousness. Where being conscious is the objective attribute, knowledge and perception are its modes or actualities. Together, both of these are called *upayoga*. — Varni 2012: 428

This way, having an interest in metaphysics is a part of knowing, which is the innate nature of consciousness.

The journey of knowledge and perception takes one towards the lighter kārmic baggage, which eventually cleanses the soul.

> Pure consciousness can perceive the objects of knowledge. As it does not require any medium for comprehension.
> — Mahaprajna 2003: 189

The type of knowledge that does not require the medium of senses and mind is known as direct knowledge (*pratyakṣa-jñāna*). Interestingly, each of the substances of the entire universe, with its past, present and future, and in all its modes and perceptions, falls into the ambit of direct knowledge because, through this specific knowledge, the being can know all at once. When the being acquires the peak of direct knowledge, it is called *kevala-jñāna* (only knowledge) or absolute knowledge. *Kevala-jñāna* has been defined as:

> The way all events display themselves without any differentiation of past, present, and future on the projection screen. In the state of absolute knowledge, all objects of the cosmos are reflected in the pure soul. — Varni 2014a: 146

This is the kind of knowledge in which the being is able to observe

[56] *upayogo lakṣaṇam* । — 2.8

the immediate different natures of the soul and matter in each occurrence, of each substance, without the discrimination of past, present and future. What a blissful and freeing state it must be when there is nothing left to be known. This way, we conclude that knowledge about reality is freedom, which is our true nature.

The journey of knowledge and perception (enlightened world view) goes hand in hand, strengthening one another — to know is to perceive and to perceive is to know. However, Ācārya Umāsvāti has given the *sūtra*[57] where enlightened world view has been put in first place.

> The enlightened world view, enlightened knowledge and enlightened conduct are the paths to liberation. —Tatia 2011: 5

Intuition, or perception, comes before and, afterwards, the being strives to know. Tatia defines the enlightened world view as:

> The world view which sees the many and the whole as enlightened. It avoids dogmas which inhibit free and open thought. Enlightened world view is the cause, enlightened knowledge and conduct the effect. — Ibid.

The whole scenario of seeking reality revolves around the entity that is behind this seeking. Be it perception or knowledge, one is bound to ask oneself and others, who knows and perceives in the first place? In Indian philosophy, this entity is the only conscious substance among the six that constitute the universe. Ācārya Kundakunda clarifies on soul:[58]

> Know that *jīva* (soul) is without taste, invisible, without odour, without sound, imperceptible (to sensory organs or instruments), without definite shape, realizable not by any mark or symbol, and characterized by the consciousness attribute. — Aggarwal 2014: 56

The knower, as indicated in Jainism, does not have any of the

57 *samyag-darśana-jñāna-cāritrāṇi mokṣamārgaḥ* । — *Tattvārthasūtra* 1.1

58 *arasamarūpamagaṅdhamavyaktaṁ cetanāguṇamaśabdaṁ* ।
jānīhi aliṅgagrahaṇaṁ jīvamanirdiṣṭasaṁsthānaṁ ॥ — *Samayasāra* 49

properties of matter. It has no shape, size, weight or colour. Hence, it is beyond the limits of physics and falls into the ambit of metaphysics. The establishing guideline of Jainism is that the knower does not pursue physical laws, and the mind, intellect and psyche are not considered as the knower but instead viewed as the reflections of the knower.

Paras Mal Aggarwal writes

> The soul can be realized without the inference based on the sense perception, i.e. it is possible by direct experience of the soul by the soul. — 2014: 57

Knowing about consciousness helps one understand life at a deeper level, which is peaceful and belongs to absolute joy that does not ask for any outer stimulation to be happy.

One stays entangled in the practical pursuits of life, thinking that one day, all will be well; however, one never finds perpetual peace. The practicality of life provides practical knowledge or knowledge of the gross; hence, it cannot provide that whose source is abstract. Still, those who peep into the knowledge of the transcendental are rare.

> All our means of knowledge are gross and these are capable of apprehending the gross alone. We have no means of comprehending the subtle. — Mahaprajna 2010: 206

The knowledge of the subtle is gained through self-experience; once accessed, it gives insights into reality. Where occurrences of life present themselves with a deeper meaning, the solutions to problems come from a place of wisdom.

Observing the present scenario of increasing cases of self-harm, the World Health Organization (WHO) confirms "one person dies (commits suicide) every forty seconds"[59] around the world and

---

[59] "Suicide: One Person Dies Every 40 Seconds", World Health Organization 2019, <https://www.who.int/news/item/09-09-2019-suicide-one-person-dies-every-40-seconds> (accessed on 26 December 2021).

> more than 700,000 people die due to suicide every year, which makes suicide the fourth leading cause of death among 15-19-year-olds.[60]

According to the leading Indian news channel *NDTV*, "India reported an average of 381 deaths by suicide daily in 2019".[61] This is shocking, too, that "300 million people worldwide are suffering from depression"[62] till 2018. Besides suicide, mental health issues and depression, there are plenty of other causes that are harming the masses, irrespective of their age. The reason behind this is easily observable: identification of the self with that which is actually opposite in nature. In Indian culture, self-realization has always been one of the most important aims of life. Now that we are under the influence of the West, spiritual studies are the need of the hour. By contemplating on the transcendental and trying to understand the metaphysics of the workings of the cosmos, we can indeed attempt to save lives and lead them positively.

---

60 Suicide. who.int.World Health Organization, 2021. Web. <https://www.who.int/news-room/fact-sheets/detail/suicide> (accessed on 26 December 2021).

61 "Average 381 Suicides Daily in India in 2019: Data", *NDTV* 2020, <https://www.ndtv.com/india-news/average-381-suicides-daily-in-india-in-2019-data-2288951> (accessed on 26 December 2021).

62 "India is the Most Depressed Country in the World", *India Today*, 2018. https://www.indiatoday.in/education-today/gk-current-affairs/story/india-is-the-most-depressed-country-in-the-world-mental-health-day-2018-1360096-2018-10-10 (accessed on 26 December 2021).

3

Spirituality in Jainism

The Concept of Soul

As the most developed species on the planet, the purpose of *Homo sapiens* is to explore life through different perspectives as much as they can and give those explorations to the next generation. To explore the consciousness is one of them.

Spirituality can be described as knowing and experiencing one's soul. *Cambridge Dictionary of Philosophy* illustrates the soul as:

> An entity supposed to be present only in living things. Plato claimed that the soul is the immaterial component of an organism, he took the soul's immateriality as grounds for its immortality.
> — Audi 2017: 1010

The subjects of soul and spirituality transcend a particular religion or philosophy. Spiritual experiences may be subjective, but the objective behind them remains the same, i.e. to get introduced to a self, higher than the self, an abstract persona that is all-powerful, wise and can perform beyond the common belief of the individual.

Different religious philosophies have described the spirit in their own ways. However, it cannot be interpreted through words because it is a matter of realization and rationality has no role to play. Spirituality covers many aspects of human life and takes one from a moment of inner transformation towards a journey of self-reflection, where one finds oneself curious to know not only the soul, its attributes, and its journey of evolution but also the concept of God, which is the ultimate objective of existence.

Soul Substance as Jīva Dravya in Jaina Philosophy

According to Jaina philosophy, the soul, known as *jīva*, is one of the six substances that constitute the universe, which possesses the unique feature of being conscious. It is neither a part of a collective consciousness nor created by a supernatural power. Each soul is on its journey of parallel evolution and devolution, according to its *bhāva* (good or bad thoughts, emotions, feelings, etc.). It has been bound in the cycle of cause and effect (*karma*) since time immemorial; at the same time, each *jīva* is capable of breaking this cycle through the trio of right world view, right knowledge and right conduct, where world view and knowledge are its innate, inseparable attributes.

Ācārya Kundakunda describes consciousness in his text *Pañcāstikāya:*[1]

> The soul substance is conscious, with knowledge and perception (intuition) as its innate attributes. It is God. It is the doer of *karma* and endures its repercussions. It moulds its shape according to the body it resides in, is incorporeal, and is always associated with *karma*.
>
> —Jalaj 2016: 33

The word *jīva* denotes consciousness that has *upayoga* (perception and knowledge) as its integral attribute. It is called God because, through its free will, it can break the cycle of cause and effect. It can do so as it has access to the key of the trio of right perception, right knowledge and right conduct. It is that which can initiate a stir into the non-living matter in the form of its actions and in turn suffers or enjoys their reactions. Just like oil occupies the whole

---

1 *jīva iti bhavati cetayitopayogaviśeṣitaḥ prabhuḥ kartā* ı
bhoktā ca dehamātro na hi mūrtaḥ karmasaṁyuktaḥ ıı — 27

body of a specific seed, even the soul substance occupies the whole body in which it has been manifested; be that of an elephant or an ant or even a unicellular being like amoeba. At the same time, it is abstract and can never be traced through even the most developed equipment as it falls beyond the ambit of five senses and the mind. Hence, it can only be experienced by the self.

A question now arises in one's mind about how and why the soul should be counted as a substance, as it is already separated by the rest of the five on the basis of its unique feature of being conscious. Jaina thinkers have clarified each query efficiently. To be counted as a substance, the specific existence must follow three requisitions as a universal law. Ācārya Umāsvāti[2] clarifies, "origination, cessation and persistence constitute existence" (Tatia 2011: 135). Each moment, subtle change is happening in each of the entities of the universe. With each passing unit of time, a new mode gets germinated in each existent, which causes its older mode to die off. Interestingly, even during this continuity of commencement and termination, there is perseverance in each entity, which allows the specific entity to keep its individual existence and substancehood intact. According to the philosophy of Jainism, these are the terms to be fulfilled by a specific to be counted as a substance and the consciousness does so.

Characteristics of the Soul

Each substance of the cosmos can be observed without and known through realization from within. However, one must be philosophical to have a clearer perception of consciousness and non-living matter. Even the basic building blocks of each material object are impossible to trace through any equipment, regardless of how advanced it is. The only conscious entity of the universe, the soul, has some prominent characteristics as described in the ancient texts of the philosophy of Jainism. These characteristics can be observed easily, as each human experiences them.

---

2 *utpād-vyaya-dhrauvyayuktaṁ sat* । — *Tattvārthasūtra* 5.30

As,[3]

> sentience is the defining characteristic of the soul. The soul is never bereft of sentience, however feeble and indistinct this may be in undeveloped organisms. — Tatia 2011: 39

Along with sentience, consciousness can be identified through its ability to perceive and know. Each living entity, irrespective of how underdeveloped it is, perceives and knows, to some extent, whether saving itself from upcoming danger or searching for its food. Even unicellular beings like

> amoebas become aware of dark spots before they come into contact with them, just as they become aware of beams of light before encountering them. — Schaeffer 1917: 61

Even the less developed trees know how to cook their food. The soul is distinguished from other souls based on its knowledge states, indicating the kārmic baggage a specific consciousness carries.

Each action gives way to the creation of causes and effects; this duo of (creating) cause and (enduring its) effect decides the journey of the soul in the form of *karma*. Thus, each being has its individual kārmic baggage to deal with. *Karma* lays the foundation of the states that differentiate consciousness from other substances. The text on reality mentions:[4]

> The states that distinguish the soul from other substances are those that: (i) are due to the suppression of the deluding *karma*, (ii) are due to the elimination of the eight types of *karma*, (iii) are mixed because of the partial elimination and partial suppression of the four destructive *karmas*, (iv) are due to the rising of the eight types of *karma*, (v) constitute the innate nature of the soul.
> — Tatia 2011: 33

The play of the soul and *karma* has continuously existed since

---

3 *upayogolakṣaṇam* । — *Tattvārthasūtra* 2.8

4 *aupaśamikar-kṣāyikau bhāvau miśraś ca jīvasya svatattvam audāyika-pariṇāmikau ca* । — Ibid. 2.1

the beginning of time. Knowledge is the inseparable attribute of consciousness and *karma* is observably enacted through different states of knowledge only, which either prevents or helps the soul from accessing its true nature. In its worldly career, consciousness appears to be suppressing some *karma*. On the other hand, according to its intellect, it can often be observed getting rid of its kārmic baggage. Hence, it keeps having partial suppression and partial elimination of *karma* (see Karma Philosophy).

Observing people in one's surroundings, one analyses that each of us, despite sharing the same attributes of perception and knowledge, is still on our respective individual journeys. Each has his destiny with his independent kārmic luggage that is decided by the choices one made, the reactions one had given in the past, and what one does at present shapes the course of their near and distant future.

Despite this immeasurable disparity among all manifestations of the soul,

> in the absolute sense, the soul has only one characteristic, *cetanā* (consciousness). The levels of development of consciousness of soul are different and so each individual in the world is different from other. — Tater 2009: 22

Collectively, humans stand on the highest step of evolution. However, each of us has a different past and will have a different future.

At the same time, it is mysterious and mesmerizing how beautifully the universe works and how efficiently our ancestors have accommodated those workings in the form of texts. Being the most evolved species on the planet, we can know the best and perceive the absolute, which is liberating.

SELF-REALIZATION: THE KEY TO EVOLUTION

I asked the immeasurable ocean, "How vast are you?".
He replied, "Unlike you, I know my grandeur".

Abraham Lincoln, the sixteenth president of the United States uttered the follwing lines in one of his best-known speeches in the history of the world: "To the people, by the people, for the people" (Grover 2020) in favour of democracy. Similarly, in the context of an individual's consciousness, the same statement can be rephrased as "to the soul, by the soul, for the soul", as the soul can only be known to itself, by itself and for the soul itself. Paras Mal Aggarwal writes:

> The soul can be realized without the inference based on the sense perception, i.e. it is possible by direct experience of the soul by the soul.
>
> — 2014: 57

Ācārya Kundakunda clarifies the characteristics of the soul further by mentioning that it is beyond the realm of senses and mind. Despite being abstract in nature, it has an existence and can only be realized. He writes in *Samayasāra:*[5]

> Know that *jīva* (soul) is without taste, invisible, without odour, without sound, imperceptible (to sensory organs or instruments), without definite shape, realizable not by any mark or symbol, and characterized by the consciousness attribute (*cetanā*).
>
> — Ibid.: 56

Often, we find ourselves so much occupied with the physical world, with rationale, that we tend to ignore the things we feel from deep within. These things can portray themselves as a subtle, abstract voice that we hear in our alone time, in our times of adversity, that leads us like no one can. However, there is no rational clarification of this voice; only a realization, and lo, one knows the answer about how to move ahead. This realization brings peace, calms one down and prepares one to be confident, irrespective of what happens in one's life.

---

5 *arasamarūpamagaṁdhamavyaktaṁ cetanaguṇamaśabdaṁ* ।
jānīhi aliṅgagrahaṇaṁ jīvamanirdiṣṭasaṁsthānaṁ ॥ — 49

Renowned German scholar Robert Zydenbos writes:

> In Jaina path of self-realization the consciousness in general is enhanced. The shedding of *karma* means that the inherent characteristics of the soul manifest themselves to an ever-greater extent.
> — Zydenbos 2006: 57

Life's journey is about accessing one's true nature and a being can do so by shedding off unnecessary kārmic baggage. For example, anger does more harm than good, as do other emotions like pride, greed, delusion, hatred and many others. With the passing of life, as one grows older, one tends to ponder these on one's own and, hence, one shapes one's perception on this basis. This way, we analyse that one moves closer to one's real essence with age.

The same example can also be applied to one's quest for knowledge, where, with age, one finds oneself attracted towards the ancient wisdom that answers questions which the practical teachings of life do not offer. This way, we find that each being evolves even during his lifetime because throughout one's life, one's perception keeps getting clearer and one dies with a better perception than with which one was born. Hence, in a way, each lifetime brings one closer to one's real nature, or, in philosophical words, the soul steps towards its characteristics with each passing life.

Considering knowledge,

> a small minority of scientists, including Nobel Prize winning physicist Eugene Wigner, took the position that measurement implies some sort of consciousness. Only a conscious person or an entity, they argued, can perform a measurement.
> — Kaku and Thompson 1995: 49

Measurement is inculcated in everyone's life irrespective of the work one does, be it household chores, building skyscrapers, covering far-off distances, losing weight or be it one's quest to search for the reality. Not only that but also we notice that each being, despite having lesser developed brains, is able to measure. For example, even a dog calculates in his brain first before getting up from one place to take a few steps to sit on the other and so do all the other beings. We see that in the root of "being able to measure" is one's ability to know. Even this finding takes us to the characteristic of the consciousness, which is knowledge.

With the right knowledge, the perception of the *jīva* (soul) becomes more precise, and it keeps getting purer and moving closer to its true nature. Also, gaining perception and knowledge unlocks the infinite spiritual joy and energy.

> The purer the *jīva*, the higher its levels of knowledge, perception, bliss and energy will become. — Mardia and Rankin 2013: 46

Even a unicellular being evolves through its knowledge to save itself from danger and to seek food to satisfy its hunger. A tree, despite not being able to move, knows how to make its food. A rice worm shrinks itself when danger is around. We can see an ant helping another ant in times of need. Even these tiny actions take underdeveloped beings further up the ladder of evolution. Humans have comparatively lighter kārmic matter (the degree may vary greatly), but those are rare who have experienced a spiritual awakening in their lives through tapping into their higher self to start their journey towards the upliftment of the soul. This may be called the purification of the soul; when consciousness continuously moves ahead to gain newer insights and knowledge, it evolves by leaps and bounds.

Beginningless association of the living (JĪVA) and the non-living (Karma)

The cosmos is an incessant play of two substances: one conscious and abstract, and the other non-living and materialistic. Right perception is realizing the opposite nature of the two.

Be it the favourable or unfavourable circumstances of one's life, the *karma* theory leads the quest of all the queries about how, when, why and where. However, like other researches, this research also starts with a hypothesis. As at the beginning of the journey of knowledge, we can only access consciousness by studying and analysing that which is contrary to its nature. "The soul exists in contamination with kārmic matter, and it longs to be purified" (Mardia and Rankin 2013: 58), for it yearns for its true nature. Ācārya Kundakunda mentions:[6]

> There are three forms of the *upayoga* associated with *moha*. These are false belief, ignorance, and vowlessness. It is to be understood that these three exist from the beginningless time.
>
> — Aggarwal 2014: 93

As we know, *upayoga* is the perception and knowledge attributes of the soul; throughout its evolution, attachment and aversion one word for these two emotions is *moha* (delusion) are not only associated with it but have also clouded it in three ways. They are false belief (considering right as wrong and the other way around), ignorance (inability to have the right knowledge about reality) and vowlessness (inability to step ahead on the path of righteousness). Through these, the consciousness is bound with *karma*. The obvious question that now arises in the mind of a researcher is: Since when are the soul and *karma* united? Ācārya Kundakunda suggests that this communion has been since time immemorial. The consciousness and the material particles, both, have been in this relationship since eternity.

A substance can neither be created nor destroyed; hence, be it the living or the non-living, they have been eternally present. As each being has always been here, it has continuously evolved and travelled from being unicellular to being the most developed form, which is human. This can be seen as either beauty or a dilemma, as the soul can evolve only because of its association with that substance, which is the opposite in nature. Once the consciousness understands that this opposite substance needs to be eliminated to advance on its spiritual journey, it embarks on the journey to end this beginningless association by breaking the shackles of kārmic

6 *upayogasyānādayaḥ pariṇāmāsrayo mohayuktasya* ।
mithyātvaṅjñānaṁviratibhāvaśca jñātavyaḥ ॥ — *Samayasāra* 89

bondage and stepping out of the cycle of cause and effect. This is but the essence of all quests.

The next question arises — how do we move on the path of discriminating these two? A few other forms of material *karma* come into the scenario to solve this dilemma, known as "the seven categories of truth". Even the subtlest of activities of the consciousness, in the form of thoughts, emotions, etc., cause attraction of the kārmic particles towards itself. This process is known as *āsrava* (inflow) of kārmic matter. The next category is known as *bandha*, which is the binding of those particles with the soul. As the being evolves, it starts to contemplate how this binding or accumulation of material *karma* can be stopped. This leads to *saṁvara* (stopping the inflow) of the kārmic matter. Now, the being starts making efforts and adopts ways to halt this cycle of cause and effect. Once it succeeds in *saṁvara*, it is left with the previously accumulated *karma*. To get rid of them, the being is now supposed to put in some effort; these are known as *nirjarā* (shedding of *karma*). Once all the piled-up *karmas* are shed, the being becomes absolutely free from the cycle of cause and effect. This state is called *mokṣa* (emancipation or liberation). All Indian philosophies depict *mokṣa* as the ultimate aim of the soul.

Fourteen Guṇasthānas: the ladder of spiritual exaltation

> *There is ignorance, and there is reality. There is a ladder that goes from prior to the latter. Every soul is either climbing, descending, or stationed at one of the rungs. Each soul can reach the top and be God.*

Irrespective of our caste, creed, gender, age or financial status, some realities remain the same for each of us. As human beings, we all deal with varied degrees of positive or negative emotions at all times. Sometimes, we suppress some sentiments and, at other times, we deal with them with such efficiency that we win over them forever. With the passage of life, one's perception of reality usually gets clearer. Each of us has some commonalities not only in terms of materialistic possessions but also in mental, emotional and spiritual efficiency. Each soul is a candidate for spiritual evolution.

> An aspirant ascends the stages of spiritual development either by subsidence (*upaśama*) or by annihilation (*kṣaya*) of *karmans*.
>
> — Bhargava 2020: 436

Throughout the journey of countless lifetimes, sometimes the soul keeps wandering, and at the other, it finds some peace, whereas, at some, it degrades. To solve this dilemma of wandering and settling, the Jaina thinkers have given the concept of the spiritual ladder, which has fourteen rungs and wraps the journeys of all souls.

The fourteen *guṇasthānas* have been described in the philosophy of Jainism as,

> due to the rise (*udaya*), subsidence (*upaśama*), annihilation (*kṣaya*), annihilation-cum-subsidence (*kṣayopaśama*) of the related *karma* of delusion and wrong perception (*darśanamohanīyādi*), each being goes through different emotions/expressions/sentiments, which designate the being in any one of these states. These states have been named *guṇasthānas* by the omniscients. — Varni 2014a: 246

Each *guṇasthāna* has been given a name in the text *Samaṇa Suttam*:[7]

> There are fourteen stages in the path of gradual spiritual development, which are as follows: (1) false belief, (2) failing from right faith, (3) mixture of right faith and wrong faith, (4) vowels right faith, (5) partial observance of vows, (6) non-vigilant observance of vows, (7) vigilant observance of vows, (8) unique condition of bliss, which has not been experienced before, (9) constant thought-activity (that is meditation), (10) slightest attachment, (11) subsided delusion, (12) destroyed delusion, (13) omniscient with activities, and (14) omniscient

---

[7] *mithyātvaṁ sāsādanaḥ miśraḥ aviratasamyaktvaḥ ca deśaviratāśca* ।
virataḥ pramattaḥ itaraḥ apūrvaḥ anivṛttiḥ sūkṣmaśca ॥ 547 ॥

upaśantaḥ kṣīṇamohaḥ saṁyogīkevalījinaḥ ayogī ca ।
caturdaśaguṇasthānāni ca krameṇa siddhāḥ ca jñātavyāḥ ॥ 548 ॥

> without activity. It should be understood that emancipation is attained in stages. — Bhargava 2020: 443

These stages encapsulate the whole (beginningless) journey of a specific soul.

1. ***Mithyādṛṣṭi guṇasthāna*** (false belief), "is a state of absolutely perverted attitude" (Bhargava 2020: 443), with unquestionably no contemplation about the fundamental nature of things.

> It is a state of a person who is totally ignorant of the higher possibilities of existence that he can achieve. — Jain 2014: 39-40

Not only that but also a state where one considers right as wrong and vice versa; the religious fanaticism we see around, be it under the name of Allāh, Jesus, Rāma or Mahāvīra, is the simplest and the clearest example of this *guṇasthāna* when one has a prejudiced point of view, contaminated by the wrong conditioning of the mind. Such a person is never open to discussions and sticks to his biased opinions about a certain philosophy

> thus, succumbs into accepting all its rituals, traditions, and rules without intellectually evaluating the logic and science behind them. — Ibid.: 41

At this rung of the ladder, a person does not contemplate the fundamental nature of things, how the universe works, the objective of life and similar probing questions.

When one observes the masses, one figures out that a significant part of the population, probably including oneself, is standing at this step. Ironically, most of us, lifetime after lifetime, only reside at this. However, one subtle question that arises beneath the innumerous layers of ignorance to know about oneself initiates the spiritual journey of a specific being. For example, someone's death can inaugurate a spiritual query about the fundamental nature of things.

2. ***Sāsvādana-samyagdṛṣṭi guṇasthāna*** (failing from right faith): The journey that starts from the first rung, which clarifies a few

doubts of the seeker about the objective reality, takes one straight to the fourth *guṇasthāna* of right perception. However, the spiritual journey is not about constant rise; here, downfall is not only inevitable but also a kind of necessity to experience the reality with even more clarity/strength. That is why this stage is linked with the fourth stage, as the one who falls from the fourth rung to the first can do so through the second rung.

> During this process, the soul experiences a slight glimpse of right insight — a state which a soul experiences only in very high realms of spirituality. —Jain 2014: 46-47

However, as it experiences something new and afresh, it starts to doubt its reality. Hence, it stays in the higher dimensions of bliss for a very short time, generates doubt and, as a result, falls back again to the first *guṇasthāna*. Still, to further clarify, the Jaina thinkers have described the second *guṇasthāna* for only those who have tasted the bliss and fallen back. Whereas those who are at the first rung and have never experienced the self stay at the first only. This is why "this is a stage not of development but that of degradation" (Bhargava 2020: 438).

3. *Samyag-mithyādr̥ṣṭi guṇasthāna* (mixture of right faith and wrong faith): It is a stage of confusion and uncertainty. After tasting the sweetness of bliss through self-realization, the soul falls down from the fourth rung to the second and then ascends to the third, still unclear about the possibilities it can achieve. "It is a mixed state of affairs. Where right belief and wrong belief coexist" (Jain 2014: 51). This state is compared to tasting the curd with sugar, which is neither sweet nor sour. At this stage,

> the soul remains indifferent to truth. It neither believes nor disbelieves it. After this stage, the soul may ascend to true belief or may descend to false belief. — Bhargava 2020: 439

For example, experiencing a state of excitement and withdrawal at the same time about a specific thing can be compared to this state.

4. *Avirata-samyagdr̥ṣṭi guṇasthāna* (vowless right faith): In the journey of life, despite facing immense conflicts and traumas, one may arrive at a peaceful conclusion that becomes the ascending track and stays with one throughout one's life. Similarly, in the journey of the soul's evolution, this state assures an upward journey for the aspirant.

> An aspirant having a firm belief in truth attains this stage. However, the aspirant is not able to observe any moral vows. Therefore, he is called *avirata*. —Bhargava 2020: 439

This state promises that the aspirant has come on the right track and, irrespective of the hurdles on the path, will sooner or later ascend the ladder of spirituality.

This is also,

> the first time, it steps out of its animalistic instincts and starts its journey upward. It is at this point that the soul actually attains humanity in the true sense of the word. —Jain 2014: 69

Now, the being gradually starts to ponder its actions and the kind of causes it creates. With the passage of time, the person becomes more and more mindful of his own essence and how he can achieve the absolute. However, despite being aware of his ability to access the higher realms of existence, his conduct is not strong enough to limit himself to create fewer causes. Hence, this stage is known as *avirata*, which indicates that the being is unable to take any ethical vow.

5. *Deśasaṁyata guṇasthāna* (partial observance of vows): This stage is the beginning of conscious control over one's passions and desires. One's quest for freedom from the mind and sensory pleasures strengthens as one knows how important it is to win over them in order to attain absolute bliss. It is a "declaration of freedom, by oneself, from oneself, and for oneself" (ibid.: 83). This stage is also known as *deśa virakta* (defining one's boundaries) (ibid.: 84). On one's journey of seeking truth, one observes, analyses and experiments with different thoughts and ideas. Slowly, with no outer influence and by its own free will, the being moves ahead and ascends the spiritual ladder towards freedom by deciding the boundaries of its own actions. "Here the stoppage of *karmans* begins. The aspirant takes partial vows" (Bhargava 2020: 439) that are in harmony with nature and the whole cosmos.

6. ***Pramattasaṁyata guṇasthāna*** (non-vigilant observance of vows), also known as the state of uncontrolled subconscious.

> The seeker in this stage is equipped with all virtuous qualities possible for a human, but still sometimes fails in his conduct, either visibly or invisibly (i.e. in the mind or dreams).
>
> — Jain 2014: 92

One's outer activities may start to feel harmonious, peaceful and wise; however, it is not easy to get rid of the inner vices that lie idle in one's subconscious and visit one occasionally. They can be subtle emotions like greed, fear, doubt, annoyance and pride or even a desire to attain the highest rung of the evolutionary ladder. But even these subtle activities create causes that keep the soul on this step. However, the being attains that level of wisdom that strengthens the faith in the solitariness and temporariness of the journey. Hence, to invigorate the trust further,

> the aspirant relinquishes all social obligations and joins the order of mendicants to devote his entire time and energies to the supreme goal. — Bhargava 2020: 440

7. ***Apramattasaṁyata guṇasthāna*** (vigilant observance of vows), also known as "the state of subconscious controlled" (Jain 2014: 93). At the seventh rung of the spiritual ladder, the aspirant succeeds in maintaining his awareness at all times (be it in sleep or while awake), in all circumstances (be it favourable or vice versa). Each of his actions is done with utmost awareness.

> His subconscious mind totally ceases to exist and he achieves absolute consciousness in all his actions. — Ibid.

Now, the person has the task of dealing with the subtler soul-soiling emotions that still attract the *karmas* towards the soul.

> In this stage the aspirant tries to overcome even the milder passions and is always struggling against them.
>
> — Bhargava 2020: 440

Even in a constant meditative state, the subtle emotions of anger, pride or any other, may visit the seeker, no matter how mild they are. In this stage, the being deals with them and tries to overcome them in an absolute manner.

8. *Nivṛttibādara guṇasthāna* (state of bliss), also known as *apūrvakaraṇa* which literally means "happening of something that has never happened before" (Jain 2014: 110). The aspirant ascends another step on the spiritual ladder, winning over even the milder emotions. It is a peaceful state of being where there is absolutely no feeling of annoyance or longing for something or self-glorification; it is just a blissful, meditative state.

> A transcendental state of mind that occurs only when a seeker attains a state of no-mind. — Ibid.: 109

In the process of evolution, the attainment of mind (by a specific being) is considered very special and unique, as the mind allows a being to differentiate between right and wrong. However, too much identification with the same becomes painful for the soul and it keeps wandering into the cycle of cause and effect. At this step, the soul steps out of its long relationship with the mind by identifying its real essence. And the moment the mind stops thinking, the speech and actions of the being (which are anyway limited by this stage), the primary reasons for the creation of causes, become constrained.

> The soul comes out successful in the struggle going on in the seventh *guṇasthāna*. Here, anger and vanity disappear.
>
> — Bhargava 2020: 440

9. *Anivṛtti-sāmparāya guṇasthāna* (constant thought-activity), which means now the aspirant is able to maintain a consistent mental state and not a state where he was dealing with frequent changes. "It is a state of transcendence" (Jain 2014: 118) and, at this rung, the seeker goes beyond the constricted boundaries of doctrine and "rises above religion and attains true humanity" (Jain 2014: 118). He travels beyond concepts and labels, and can now access his pure essence, the infinite ocean of perception, knowledge, bliss and power, from within and without. After discarding the emotions of anger and pride in the eighth *guṇasthāna*, in this stage

> deceit disappears; also, the struggle for spiritual progress comes to an end and his progress becomes automatic.
>
> — Bhargava 2020: 440

Now there is no looking back; the seeker has entered the one-way track,

> the Godhood is now just forty-eight minutes away, a time span named as *antar-muhūrtta* in Jaina theology. — Jain 2014: 117

10. *Sūkṣma-sāmparāya guṇasthāna* (slightest attachment), in this stage

> only a subtle greed, in the form of subtle attachment of soul with body, remains. — Bhargava 2020: 441

Now, the aspirant has to deal with very subtle passive desires. All desires, attachments and emotions of love and hatred are the result of the mind. By this stage, the conscious mind and subconscious mind have been eliminated. However,

> apart from the conscious and the subconscious minds, there is another layer of mind far deeper than the earlier two. Psychologists call this third layer as reflexes. — Jain 2014: 121

Reflexes are, "involuntary and nearly instantaneous movements in response to a stimulus",[8] at this rung the aspirant is worthy of controlling his reflexes. This way his body movements along with

---

[8] "Reflexes", Spinal reflex/The reflex Arc. Physio-pedia, <https://www.physio-pedia.com/Reflexes> (accessed on 28 February 2022).

his thought activities, become less and less frequent, and he remains constantly in a deep meditative state.

11. ***Upaśāntamohanīya guṇasthāna*** (subsided delusion): Delusion (*mohanīya karma*) is known to be the most dangerous reason for consciousness to be bound in the cycle of creating causes and enduring their effects.

> *Jina* (the omniscient) compares a seeker at this stage to water mixed with *kaṭaka* fruit-seeds to achieve purity. —Jain 2014: 125

Kaṭaka (*Strychnos potatorum*) is a cleaning nut because it instantly purifies water. At this stage, the aspirant appears to have entered the one-way track towards Godhood; however, deep within, he still deals with some conflicts. This is why this state is compared with clear water, the mud of which has not been removed; rather, it has settled down at the bottom, and even a mild stir can cause the mud to dirty the water again.

Hence, one last time, delusion strikes back in this *guṇasthāna* and obstructs the aspirant's spiritual journey.

> Soul in this *guṇasthāna* does not go further. As aspirant from this *guṇasthāna* descends either to the sixth or the fifth or the fourth or the first *guṇasthāna*. —Bhargava 2020: 441

This is how nasty delusion is! However, this rung on the ladder also depicts that the seeker has not dealt with his kārmic baggage efficiently and has suppressed some of his emotions to climb the ladder quickly. There can neither be any jostle nor a shortcut to ascend this ladder; hence, the seeker will be held over inevitably to go further. It indicates that he has yet to learn some lessons. However, it is interesting to know that this is not the end, as the consciousness has already tasted the bliss and has gone through the fourth rung, which is the right perception. Therefore, within a certain period, the soul again ascends the ladder to attain liberation.

12. ***Kṣīṇakaṣāyachadamastha-vītarāga guṇasthāna or kṣīṇa moha*** (destroyed delusion):

> In this stage, the *mohanīya* (delusion), which is the main obstruction, is completely destroyed. In the last *samaya* of this stage, five types of *jñānāvarṇī*, *darśanāvarṇī*, and *antarāya karmans* are completely annihilated. — Bhargava 2020: 441

The *karma* of delusion keeps the soul away from attaining the pinnacle of spirituality and, the moment it is destroyed, the very next event that happens within one unit of time is the destruction of the knowledge - obscuring, perception - obscuring *karma*s and the *karma* that causes obstruction (of any form) on the journey to attain liberation. Comparing this stage with the eleventh *guṇasthāna* clarifies that now the aspirant has no residual, even the slightest of (kārmic) dust in any form.

> Such a person is like a lake whose water has become totally pure. There is no dirt left over at its bottom either. — Jain 2014: 153

13. ***Sayogakevalī guṇasthāna*** (omniscient with activities), also known as "the state of the supreme soul with body" (ibid.: 156). By this stage, the aspirant has already won over all four *ghātī karma*s (destructive *karmas*): knowledge obscuring, perception obscuring, delusion and obstruction. However, there is still something that needs to be taken care of. Ācārya Kundakunda writes on the essence of soul:

> Wrong belief, vowlessness (*avirati*), *kaṣāya* and *yoga* are four common doors for *kārmika* influx (*pratyaya*). Indeed, these *pratyayas* are said to be responsible for *kārmika* bonding.
> — Aggarwal 2014: 116

At this rung, the soul is absolutely free from three out of four causes of bondage (*pratyaya*), i.e. *mithyātva* (wrong belief), vowlessness (*avirati*) and soul-soiling emotions (*kaṣāya*). Only the fourth door through which *karmas* incessantly enter into the territory of soul, *yoga*, i.e. the (subtlest) activities of mind, speech and action, remains. However,

> the four infinities (*ananta-jñāna*, *ananta-vīrya*, *ananta-darśana* and *ananta-sukha*) are obtained. — Bhargava 2020: 441

This *guṇasthāna* is also the state of the *arhanta*, which can be understood as the pinnacle of humanhood or beinghood. The topmost rung on the ladder of evolution, at the end of this stage, the soul breaks free from the beginningless cycle of cause and effect, and attains the fourteenth *guṇasthāna*, Godhood.

14. *Ayoga-kevalī guṇasthāna* (omniscient without activity): This is the stage of omniscient who has transcended *yoga*. As soon as the four *aghātī karmas* (non-destructive *karmas*) of *vedanīya* (feeling of pleasure and pain), *nāma* (body-making), *gotra* (social status) and *āyu* (age) complete their time; it only takes

> as much time as is required to pronounce five short vowels. At the end of this period the soul leaves the embodied state forever and goes straight above, to the end of the universe, to enjoy its inherent blissfulness forever. — Bhargava 2020: 442

Ayogakevalī means the being "whose bond between the material body and soul is annihilated" (Jain 2014: 157). Such is the beauty of beingness that each being is able to become God.

Siddha: Souls that have attained liberation (mokṣa)

> *Oh what a state!*
> *Where pervades nothing but the consciousness in its purest*
> *Infinity of knowledge, perception, bliss and power*
> *Mere imagination fills one with happiness.*

The very next state, after all the rungs on the ladder of evolution, is the state of the *siddha*, which means beings,

> who have destroyed the restriction of all eight types of *karmas*, are located at the topmost realm of the universe, and are absolute and eternal. — Varni 2014b: 323

They can be called *mukta jīvas* (liberated souls). Those who have reached the apex of evolution, and, hence, have been able to go beyond that and access their essence in the absolute sense, are the souls who have attained *mokṣa*. They have dealt with their kārmic baggage in such a way that now there is none left. They have not only stopped generating the causes but heve also shed all the accumulated kārmic matter; through this, they have stepped out of the cycle of cause and effect that is observable in birth–death–rebirth. Now, they do not belong to the realm of relativity as they have accessed the absolute. Those who have achieved so are called the liberated souls and are stationed at the crown of the universe until infinity.

This way, we see that the study of *guṇasthāna* makes one not only realize the best possibility of being human but also expresses evolution in the real sense, where evolution occurs in the soul substance first, which reflects in the physical body of that specific being later.

Mind and Body

Oh, mind, mind, mind!
Can't you stop the grind?
The soul has earned you
Through its long journey of evolution
In the beginning, you were friends
But now you need to be cleansed
You keep it bound in delusion
It has to withdraw itself
To attain liberation.

Whether it is about accomplishing a certain goal or controlling one's intense desires, one is suggested to win over the mind. For ages, man has wondered what the mind is and how it works. Some intellectuals have termed it the sixth sense in abstract form and others have termed it the soul itself.

> Mind, in the Western tradition, is the complex of faculties involved in perceiving, remembering, considering, evaluating and deciding. Mind is in some sense reflected in such occurrences

> as sensations, perceptions, emotions, memory, desires, various types of reasoning, motives, choices, traits of personality, and the unconscious.[9]

The mind decides between right and wrong, remembers situations and events, assesses different scenarios or personalities and draws conclusions.

Mind in the philosophy of Jainism

In the text on reality, Ācārya Umāsvāti mentions,[10] "those that have a mind are intelligent beings" (Tatia 2011: 46). Tatia clarifies the *sūtra* further, in his commentary on the same text:

> Intelligence or rationality means the capacity to remember the past and ponder over the future. Intelligence as a subconsciously motivated behaviour is the survival instinct concerned with acquiring food, resorting to fight or flight, sexual activity and provision for future (possessiveness). — Ibid: 46-47

A being acquires the mind through its unimaginably lengthy journey of evolution, from a unicellular, one-sensed being without a mind, to a five-sensed being with a mind when it acquires the body of a dog, lion, cow or similar animals. It keeps evolving until it attains the most developed form, by all means (in the context of the brain, body structure and mind itself), of humans. Owning the mind equips the being not only to remember the events of its journey through life but also to make sensible decisions about choosing the right partner, finding food, saving itself from danger and possessing enough to secure its future. This way, we see that the mind is not an enemy but perhaps the closest friend of a specific being. However, the problem starts when, due to its long association, the soul misidentifies the mind with itself and forgets that "consciousness is a precondition of a being" (Jung 2006: 48).

---

9 "Mind", brittanica.com, Britannica, 2022, <https://www.britannica.com/biography/Theodor-Lipps> (accessed on 20 March 2022).

10 *saṁjñināḥ samanaskāḥ* । — *Tattvārthasūtra* 2.25

Being rational, we are equipped to know not through what others believe but through what we experience ourselves about a specific object, circumstance or personality. Our experiences play the crucial role in leading our lives in the right direction, be it professional success or personal. The knowledge we gain throughout our lives is "empirical knowledge which is produced by the senses and the mind" (Tatia 2011: 14). The mind alone cannot do anything unless it is associated with the five senses, laying the foundation of our experiential cognition. Hence, the knowledge one gains throughout life is intricately woven through the mind and senses.

Types of Mind: Dravya Mana (Physical Mind) and Bhāva Mana (Abstract Mind)

However, now, the question arises of whether thoughts, emotions and all the other aspects of the mind are physical or abstract. Where do they originate in the body? In the philosophy of mind, this problem is called the mind–body problem.

> A central one in philosophy of mind concerns whether mental phenomena are physical and, if not, how are they related to the physical. — Audi 2010: 802

In the philosophy of Jainism, we find interesting solutions to this query. Varni (2014b: 269) describes the mind as "an internal sense, which is of two types: physical (*dravya*) and abstract (*bhāva*)". Here, the abstract depicts the subtle thoughts that initiate physical activities, whereas physicality indicates that the mind also exists in a physical form in the body.

Physical Mind

> Due to a certain shape, the physical mind (*dravya mana*) is a mode of non-living matter (*pudgala dravya*). — Ibid.: 270

This explains that the mind has a form dimension too. The shape and location of the mind have been described as

> that which occupies a space in the heart and has the appearance of a lotus flower with eight petals. – Verni 2014b: 270

Now, a rational mind will ask, "Then why has no one discovered the mind (as an organ) yet?" Varni provides the answer.

> It is extremely minute and cannot be observed through any of the senses. — Ibid.

This solution creates yet another dilemma in any rational mind. To find a solution, we may think of it in the following way – there are many mind-boggling facts about the human body like:

> We shed 600,000 particles of skin every hour and in one lifetime, the average person produces two swimming pools' worth of saliva.[11]

We have not known about these facts for a long period in the history of modern science. Still, as we progressed, we kept evolving in the context of our inquisitiveness and instruments. We kept researching newer phenomena of the nature of the human body, which does not mean that these happenings were not taking place earlier. Similarly, research in the field of mind is open to further inquiry. At the same time, we must keep in mind that certain realities cannot be understood through the use of mind. The mind can never find answers by the mind for the mind unless consciousness is there in the first place.

Abstract Mind

> *Bhāva mana* is an aspect of knowledge, and knowledge is the innate and inseparable attribute of the soul; the abstract mind is in immediate connection with the consciousness. — Ibid.

If there is a mind that thinks, there is also a subconscious mind, "which does a lot of the heavy lifting in the process of thinking"

---

11 "7 Mind-Blowing Facts About the Human Body", *Stamina*, 28 August 2017, <https://staminaproducts.com/blog/7-mind-blowing-facts-human-body/> (accessed on 3 April 2022).

(Stafford 2015). To climb the ladder of spiritual evolution and achieve enlightenment, one is supposed to win over the mind, the subconscious mind, along with all its layers. Even reflexes seem to be under the command of the mind, as a reflex is defined as

> an involuntary motor response, secretory or vascular, elicited shortly after a stimulus, which may be conscious or not.
>
> — Latash and Zatsiorsky 2016

Majorly the mind has been divided into two parts by the Jaina thinkers. However, modern thinkers have delved into these two and have tried to find out the unconscious mind that "stores all repressed thoughts and feelings" (Ricee 2021) and the last mind is "even beyond reflexes" (Jain 2014: 126). Carl Jung (2006: 48) indicates the abstract mind when he calls an individual the "immediate manifestation of the psyche" which again takes us closer to what Jaina thinkers have described about the mind.

Relationship between the Mind and the Soul

Who owns the mind, to whom thinking happens, or the other way around, because of whom thinking happens? It surely is a separate entity other than the mind. Modern spiritual teacher Eckhart Tolle negates the famous statement of René Descartes, "I think, therefore I am". He writes in his international best seller *The Power of Now*:

> He (Descartes) had given expression to the most basic error: to equate thinking with Being and identity with thinking.
>
> — Tolle 2001: 12

If one exists only because one can think, then what happens when one has just arrived in this world, is as clean as a slate and is completely unaware of what thinking is? Also, what happens to that thinking when one dies? We analyse:

> Thinking is only a small aspect of consciousness. Thought cannot exist without consciousness, but consciousness does not need thought. — Tolle 2001: 19

The cosmos comprises of only two substances: the living and the non-living. Both are opposite in nature and have been eternally present. The living is the conscious substance, and the non-living is that which is not conscious. The visible world is a constant play of these two, where the conscious substance manifests itself in countless forms through the non-living. They keep uniting and separating, reflecting each others' identity as their own, but never lose their real essence. In this context, we analyse that even the physical mind is made up of non-living matter. Hence, we see:

> Mind, like the soul, is not a permanent entity; it exists only when consciousness manifests as thoughts, beliefs, desires, emotions and feelings. — Kachchara 2011: Abstract

Initiation of all emotions is possible because of the perversion of the soul, due to which the related non-living (kārmic) matter converts itself into different actions. The purer the soul, the better it rids emotions and the lesser the mind influences it.

Ācārya Kundakunda distinguishes the contrast of these two substances in his *Samayasāra*[12] as:

> *Pudgala* (matter/energy) transforms into *kārmika* matter (of eight kinds) by *nimitta* of *jīva*'s actions. A *jīva* also undergoes changes by *nimitta* of *pudgala karma*. — Aggarwal 2014: 85

From the above description, we analyse that the living and the non-living act as instrumental causes for each other. For example, breaking the glass by the servant becomes the instrumental cause of anger in the owner's mind. Here, the event happened to the non-living matter enacted as an instrumental cause to initiate emotions in the soul through another non-living matter, the mind. However, the main reaction (of anger) comes from the consciousness, which again acts as the instrumental cause for the mind to retaliate through the senses.

---

12 *jīvapariṇāmahetuṁ karmatvaṁ pudagalāḥ pariṇamaṅti* ı
pudgalakarmanimittaṁ tathaiva jīvopi pariṇamati ‖ — 80

We notice that all emotions, desires, feelings of pain and joy, etc., act as bridges between the living and non-living.

> All these activities are influenced by *karma*, which is an interface between the soul and the mind. The soul perceives and knows the external world through the mind, so the perceptions made by the soul are influenced by the mind. — Kachchara 2011: Abstract

The mind is at rest until the consciousness is not involved in any activity. However, one cannot refrain from any activities because, from the day one arrives into this world, one has to use one's mind to understand things around. Which never lets one understand one's natural essence. It is the mind that gets conditioned and not the soul. This way, one's misconception of considering the mind as oneself sows the seed of mental troubles in the form of different emotions. In the context of *karma*, we see that we inevitably do something or the other with each passing unit of time. This "doing something" not only keeps the mind and consciousness involved with each other but also keeps generating causes that act as a bridge between the two.

Here the role of the brain is

> as the centre for information storage and processing, its activity is regulated by the mind, which in turn is conditioned by the soul. The conscious experience is made by the soul, not by the mind.
>
> — Ibid.

Hence, we see that the perversions of the soul condition the mind and vice versa. This parallel journey is strong enough to confuse each living being into thinking that mind itself is the consciousness. A thought is initiated in the mind and then takes shape through speech and physical action, respectively. Thus, the very first step of indulgence in the world around is possible only through the mind.

> The existence of mind is connected with its activities, when the activities cease, the mind also ceases to exist.
>
> — Kachchara 2011: 8

Meditation and self-contemplation help one minimize the constant chatter in the mind. The moment these activities stop or whittle down, the being realizes that its true essence is beyond the ambit of mind and senses.

One more fact differentiates between the soul and the mind: "The mind can have just one thought at a time" (ibid.). However, it is not the same with consciousness, as it can perceive many, simultaneously. In the state of omniscience, when the being wins over the destructive *karma*, it perceives truth as a whole and not in parts or series.

Despite the dependency of senses on the mind, we analyse that the senses are only small windows that help the being notice objects, events, etc. only in physical form. Whereas, the mind is the gateway to analyse them further in the context of right and wrong, compare them, etc., However, the primary doer sits even behind the mind, letting it take charge so much so that it starts to think it is the principal doer. Modern science and ancient philosophies both describe the mind as the faculty that makes a being rational, judgemental and emotional. But sole dependency upon the mind leads nowhere. We need to realize "that" because of which the mind comes into existence, "that" which earned the mind during its evolution. Only then can we conclude that "we all possess intuitive abilities far beyond what we realize" (Brian 2010: 42) through the mind. Researching the mind is mind-boggling, for we get stuck in rationality and logic. Carl Jung simplifies this dilemma by adding, "too much attention to external blocks the way to immediate inner experience" (2006: 49). Hence, we must realize that the mind is that servant in whose hands the soul has given the keys of life but for practical purposes only; however, it is the soul to which the journey of the absolute belongs.

Meditation

> *Meditation is recognizing the owner (soul) for whom the servant (mind) works, misapprehending itself as the owner.*

Meditation can be defined as a few moments of concentration in doing what one loves, with a satisfactory smile on one's face and a feeling of inner peace. At a basic level, this seems enough to peep into one's soul, which can eventually be practised more to reach a higher state of realization. Spirituality has an intimate connection with meditation. In today's world, the number of people in touch with meditation is relatively higher, and it keeps increasing as more and more people are introduced to various meditative techniques through different teachers. Still, very few can meditate to maintain a blissful mental state and, through that, improve their and others' lives.

Collins Dictionary defines meditation as

> the act of remaining in a silent and calm state for a period of time, so that you are more able to deal with the problems of everyday life.[13]

However, to attain higher realms of spiritual bliss, meditation is seen as a journey from the outer world to the inner to achieve the absolute. It is to know oneself to the utmost, and can also be depicted as "perceiving the soul through the soul to become the supreme soul" (Mahaprajna 2003: 100).

Meditation in the philosophy of Jainism

In the philosophy of Jainism, *dhyāna* has been described in many ways. One definition is:

> Concentration is meditation, which means becoming one with a specific idea (or image, notion, nature or sentiment) by contemplating the same. — Varni 2014a: 494

Another definition is "steadiness of overall thought process is meditation" (ibid.: 482). When one is in a specific profession, be it constructing buildings or writing a book, one focuses one's overall thinking on that specific project. During those days, one's

13 "Meditation", Collins, <https://www.collinsdictionary.com/dictionary/english/meditation> (accessed on 5 May 2022).

persona reflects one's inner state of mind, which is occupied with thoughts about one's present project. This thought process can be of worry, helplessness or any other emotion; however, it can also be of satisfaction and pleasantness. During that period, we notice a steadiness in one's overall thought process. Hence, we conclude that one is meditating upon that specific project. When we analyse one's overall life, we observe that each human being develops a specific thought process throughout one's lifetime via different experiences and occurrences. This thought process may be one of cribbing and complaining or, on the contrary, of surrender and hope.

Each thought is meditation because our mind is occupied with it, followed by our speech and actions. We discussed *yoga* earlier, which talked about the activities of this trio — *mana* (mind), *vacana* (speech) and *kāya* (physical actions). Hence, we see that just like *karma* is being performed with each passing moment, so does meditation, inevitably. For, we focus on one thing or the other at all times.

Another similar definition of meditation is:

> The stagnancy of one's cognizance in a specific object of knowledge is meditation. — Ibid.

Due to the innate, inseparable and eternal attributes of knowledge and perception, emotions like pride, anger, desires and fear are objects of knowledge for the soul. At the same time, visible objects like books, computers and glass are also objects to be known. The first category falls into the ambit of the perverted nature of consciousness, whereas the second belongs to objects with physicality. This way, we see that everything out there and within, physical and abstract, is an object of knowledge for the consciousness. Hence, contemplating anything falls under the vast subject matter of meditation. This is why, in Indian culture, one is suggested to focus one's attention and energy on positive things. Be it choosing a profession, selecting a life partner or even adopting food choices, one is advised to be mindful at all times.

Ārtta Dhyāna

It is one of the negative meditations.

> A worldly being deals with blemished thoughts twenty-four-seven. Some are caused by separation from a loved one, some by unfavourable circumstances, some by pain, and others by concern for future possessions, etc. All these thoughts are called *ārtta dhyāna*. — Varni 2012: 272

At a spiritual level, we see that all our worldly activities keep our attention bound to the worldly realm. In contrast, the realm of consciousness is much vast and divine, which stays under the layers of ignorance. When a being gets a glimpse of its real essence, he ponders beyond negative meditations.

Raudra Dhyāna

In Indian culture, one is advised to be mindful and to check one's thoughts, speech and actions at all times. The description of *raudra dhyāna* throws light on actions that are sometimes considered good, but as harmful intentions cause them, they create long-term adverse effects.

> The sentiment to boast proudly about violence, vices, etc., done by one is *raudra dhyāna*. The intent to take over other's possessions, to take pleasure in lying, thoughts of killing someone, etc., is known as *raudra dhyāna* briefly. — Varni 2014b: 407

Countless examples of this meditation can be observed in one's day-to-day life. Ethics are highly at stake in today's world, be it professional competition or rivalry among nations, so much so that one hardly gives heed to these clearly noticeable but subtle thoughts that eventually decide the course of one's life. Also, "that man who ruthlessly makes others cry inevitably does *raudra dhyāna*" (Varni 2014b).

Besides these,

> uttering cruel, rude and abusive words; dishonouring, incarcerating, threatening and punishing someone; and

> fornicating a woman forcefully, etc., are to be known as external *raudra dhyāna.* — Ibid.: 408

It is clearly observable that through such actions, the being accumulates pain-body for itself, depending upon the intent and intensity of thoughts during the execution of such actions.

Piṇḍastha Dhyāna

Assumable through its name, it is a meditation on a physical object because the word *piṇḍa* means "depth or thickness" (ibid.: 57). However, the purpose of each type of meditation is to help the seeker climb the ladder to *mokṣa.* This meditation technique suggests contemplating the soul substance by imagining one's body as the *loka* (universe) and relating different body parts to the different realms of the cosmos.

> By imagining the Meru mountain (the exact centre of the whole universe as described in the annals) in the navel, hellish dimensions in the lower parts (below the navel), all animals (from unicellular beings to five-sensed beings) in the lateral parts (of the navel). Contemplating heavens in the upper part from the navel, speculating the forehead as *siddha śilā* (the place where all liberated souls reside) and considering the uppermost part of the body (i.e. crown *cakra*) as the topmost realm of the universe, which is the state of a *siddha,* should be meditated upon. — Ibid.

Padastha Dhyāna

As indicated through its name, this meditation is

> to establish the vowels, consonants or *bīja mantras* (root *mantra*) like *oṁ hrīṁ* (ॐ ह्रीं) into their respective body parts of navel and heart and meditate upon them is *padastha dhyāna.* Through this meditation, the meditator's *upayoga* (knowledge and perception) stabilizes, and once it is practised enough, he can attain the state of absolute meditation. — Varni 2014b: 5

This is a meditation technique that focuses attention on certain alphabets and words. We see many people around chanting *mantras* and, through that, focusing their attention within. However, as soon as the aspirant can travel beyond the labels, he gets on the path to attain the absolute.

Rūpastha Dhyāna

It is to meditate upon the form of those beings who have broken free from the shackles of cause and effect, and have attained absolute freedom (*mokṣa*). And, in the process (with the purest of intent, using one's free will), sowing the seeds of that tree which gives the fruit of *mokṣa*.

> *Rūpastha dhyāna* is to contemplate the *arhanta* god. That being who is omniscient, all-giving, forever flourishing, free from diseases, eternal, unspoken, flawless, and is forever. — Ibid.: 405

The state of the *arhanta* can also be called the state of the most evolved human being.

Rūpātīta Dhyāna

Rūpātīta dhyāna and *śukla dhyāna* are synonymous. As cleared by the name, *rūpātīta* means "that which is beyond form". The higher the meditation technique is, the higher it takes the aspirant from the limited world of physicality to the vast blissfulness of the abstract, from the natural to the supernatural.

> To meditate upon the pure nature of the soul, which is sheer knowledge and perception, is beyond any colour, taste, odour or physicality, which is the state of a liberated soul, i.e. *siddha* god, is *rūpātīta dhyāna*. — Ibid.: 406

Sāmāyika Dhyāna

> To neither have attachment nor aversion to happiness and sorrow, gain and loss, desirable and undesirable; rather, to have a sentiment of a spectator who only knows and witnesses all these with equanimity, always staying immersed in one's own soul, is *sāmāyika*. Also, absolute resignation from the activities of mind, speech, and actions (*yoga*) is *sāmāyika*. — Varni 2014b: 413

This is the meditation advised for saints and householders to practise equanimity. It is the simplest and most important technique for proceeding onto the path of spiritual enlightenment and keeping one's kārmic baggage lighter. Imagine if we start performing *karma* with the intent of neither gain nor loss; what would we collect for ourselves? All soul-soiling emotions would leave us for good, for there would be no attachment or aversion, which eventually gives rise to anger, pride, delusion, greed and the rest of emotions.

Dharma Dhyāna

Seeing the boundless sphere of meditation that covers an individual's whole life, it becomes necessary to differentiate between the right meditation, which takes one to higher spiritual paths and meditation with a deluded view, which keeps one bound in the cycle of cause and effect. Hence, Varni clarifies further:

> Meditation happens every moment as one's attention is always entangled with something or the other. However, due to attachment or aversion, these types of meditation are considered pestiferous. The right introspection is called *dharma dhyāna* (righteous meditation), and it is performed to achieve equanimity.
>
> —2014a: 476

The meditation that is not perverted but that which can analyse the fundamental nature of things and, hence, can take one onto greater spiritual dimensions.

In Indian culture, everyone is advised to cover that distance for which no travel is required in space and time. That is the only way of knowing oneself. One of the *sūtras* in the text on the essence of Jainism, the *Samaṇa Suttam*[14] indicates the magnificence of meditation, as described by the omniscient:

---

[14] *āruhya antarātmānaṁ bahirātmānaṁ tyaktvā trividhena* ।
dhyāyate paramātmā upadiṣṭaṁ jinavarendraiḥ ॥ 181 ॥

> Relinquishing the extrovert attitude from your mind, speech and body, realize the *antarātmā* and contemplate on the Supreme Soul (*Paramātmā*). — Bhargava 2020: 182

This *sūtra* has been simplified further as:

> Leave *bahirātmā* (outbound soul), settle in *antarātmā* (inbound soul) and contemplate on *Paramātmā* (Supreme Soul) by your mind, thoughts and body. —Jain 2014: 1

Bahirātmā is the soul that is indulged in worldly activities such as earning money, fulfilling relationships, owning materialistic possessions and desiring societal respect. In contrast, *antarātmā* is described as the inner voice of the consciousness that shows one the right way in any dilemma or adversity that one deals with in one's life. We notice that in both the outbound and inbound souls, one is inevitably using one's senses and mind. The meditation techniques show the way beyond these and suggest controlling the activities of mind, speech and actions, and knowing the purest formless dimension of oneself, the Supreme Soul (*Paramātmā*). The absolute nature of consciousness does not require the medium of mind and senses to know to whom this journey belongs in the true sense.

> Consciousness, by its very nature, is a seer. In its purest form, it does not need a medium. It is only when the mind casts its shadow on it that it needs a medium of perception. — Mahaprajna 2013: 9

Every soul is an unexplored *Paramātmā* and each being is suggested to access that God within who knows it all because knowledge is its inseparable attribute. Meditation introduces us to the inner self, which lies hidden in all of us and is beyond the outbound self. However, the exact purpose of meditation is to take the individual even beyond the inbound soul and show a glimpse of the absolute.

Śukla Dhyāna

The most pious and ultimate spiritual meditation is the *śukla dhyāna*, which takes the seeker to a stage where he has destroyed the delusion; at this stage, even the subtlest thoughts, desires, emotions, etc., leave the aspirant forever.

> *Rūpātīta dhyāna* or *śukla dhyāna* is when, during meditation, the saint is able to intently finish off the attachment (and aversion) and enter into an unwavering *samādhi*. He is able to remain as stagnant as the flame of a candle made of a gemstone. He does not even have to preclude his breathing, as it happens independently. This meditation is the direct cause of liberation. — Varni 2012: 31

Through different stages of meditation, an aspirant can attain freedom from the cycle of cause and effect, which is termed liberation (*mokṣa*) in Indian philosophies. Hence, we conclude that meditation holds the key to liberation.

Twelve Contemplations (Bārasa Aṇuvekkhā/Anuprekṣā)

Anuprekṣā means to contemplate. Every human being is suggested to ponder these twelve objective realities to prepare oneself for life, its ups and downs, and the journey beyond. Ācārya Umāsvāti throws light upon these in his text on reality.[15]

> The twelve reflections are upon impermanence, helplessness, the cycle of birth and death, solitariness, otherness of the body, impurity of the body, inflow of *karma*, inhibiting *karma*, wearing of *karma*, the nature of the cosmos, rarity of enlightenment and the lucid exposition of the doctrine. — Tatia 2011: 223

Anitya Bhāvanā (Transitoriness)

Throughout life, we often ponder the impermanent nature of things. We take birth as tiny babies and change incessantly. The world around us also continuously transforms. However, things we wrongly presume permanent, turn out to be temporary as well. For example, besides fame, money, youth, life, our relations, even the strongest building made on earth, even the gods we worship,

15 *anityā-śaraṇa-saṁsārai-katvā-nyatvā-śucitvā-srva-saṁvara-nirjarā-loka-bodhidurlabha-dharmasvākhyātattvānuciṁtanama anuprekṣāḥ* ।
— *Tattvārthasūtra* 9.7

are all transitory. Our ancient thinkers have suggested pondering what is permanent in the real sense. Ācārya Kundakunda says:[16]

> Contemplate, from the transcendental-point-of-view (*niścaya naya*), incessantly on the nature of the soul as perpetually different from the glory of the lords of the heavenly-*devas*, the other-*devas* and the humans. —Jain 2021: 12

Aśaraṇa Bhāvanā (Helplessness)

The second contemplation, suggested for every human, is upon the inability to provide shelter to the one dying along with the inefficacy to get the same for oneself at the time of death:[17]

> Certainly, in the three worlds, nothing at all — magical gems, incantations, medicines, protective gears, horses, elephants, chariots and all types of learning — can afford refuge to the dying men. —Jain 2021: 18

We observe that death happens everywhere at all times. People die around us and at a distance. Sometimes some of our near ones dies and at other some of our acquaintances leave the world. Sometimes a young child or a youth dies and at the other an old person. We can all reflect on this and see that there is absolutely no one who can save the dying one. Surely, we can do our *puruṣārtha*, but only to a minimal extent.

Ekatva Bhāvanā (Solitariness)

In his text on twelve contemplations, *Bārasa Aṇuvekkhā*, Ācārya Kundakunda states further:[18]

---

16 *paramārthena tu ātmā devāsuramanujarājavividhaiḥ* ।
vyatiriktaḥ sa ātmā śāśvata iti cintayennityaṁ ॥ — *Bārasa Aṇuvekkhā* 7

17 *maṇimaṅtrauṣadhirakṣā hayagajarathāśca sakalavidyāḥ* ।
jīvānāṁ na hi śaraṇaṁ triṣu lokeṣu maraṇasamaye ॥ — ibId. 8

18 *ekaḥ karoti karma eko hiṇḍati ca dīrghasaṁsāre* ।
eko jāyate mrīyate ca tasya phalaṁ bhukta ekaḥ ॥
— *Bārasa Aṇuvekkhā* 14

> Alone does the worldly-soul perform (auspicious or inauspicious) *karma*, alone does it wander in this perpetual (beginningless) world, alone does it take birth, alone does it die; only alone does it enjoy the fruit of own *karma*. — Jain 2021: 28

In our youth, we tend to oppose these kinds of statements. However, as time passes, we grow up, and with our own experiences and observations, we conclude that each of us is alone in this world. For example, someone nearby may get an incurable disease, and despite the best efforts of the family, the person cannot be saved.

Anyatva Bhāvanā (Distinctness)

A glass is different from a book and a book is different from a tree. We analyse that even one glass is different from the other glass and so on. Similarly, each living being is distinct from the other. Even if each soul shares the same attributes, no one can share the other's individuality. Ācārya Kundakunda writes:[19]

> The mother, the father, the brother, the son, the wife and all kinsfolk do not have (real) oneness with the worldly-soul (*jīva*); all these relations hinge on self-interest. — Ibid.: 40

No matter how close someone is to another person, it is not possible at all not to expect something in a relationship. Each kinship is based on some or the other self-interest. For example, when someone dies, his near ones cry, saying, "Now what will happen to me? How would I survive in this world?". No one says, "The one departed was an individual who moved ahead onto his individual journey". Hence, we see these reflections prepare us for the journey of life.

---

19 *mātṛpitṛsahodaraputrakalatrādibandhusaṅdohaḥ* ।
jīvasya na sambandho nijakāryavaśena vartate ॥
— *Bārasa Aṇuvekkhā 21*

Saṁsāra Bhāvanā (Transmigration)

To reflect upon the nature of the cycle of birth–death–rebirth is *saṁsāra bhāvanā*. Ācārya Kundakunda elaborates:[20]

> The soul (*jīva*) which has vanquished transmigration (*saṁsāra*) is worth accepting (*upādeya*); this should be the subject of contemplation. The soul which is still experiencing worldly miseries is worth discarding (*heya*); this should be the subject of contemplation. —Jain 2021: 56

In the philosophy of Jainism, the emphasis is upon whom to worship and whom not. For enlightenment, the aspirant is suggested to look up to only those who have attained liberation, those who have travelled from the outbound soul (*bahirātmā*) to the inbound soul (*antarātmā*) and eventually have attained the Supreme Soul (*Paramātmā*). The journey is to find the reason for one's constant wandering into the different realms of the world in different bodies, knowing that an ultimate dimension exists, and starting one's journey to attain so.

Loka Bhāvanā the Universe

To contemplate the nature of the cosmos in the context of roaming around in its different dimensions according to one's *karma* is the *loka bhāvanā*. Ācārya Kundakunda describes:[21]

> The worldly-soul (*jīva*) in which manifests the inauspicious-cognition (*aśubhopayoga*) plunges into states-of-existence (*gati*) either in infernal-region (*naraka*) or among plant-and-animal (*tiryañca*). The soul in which manifests the auspicious-cognition (*śubhopayoga*) gets to enjoy pleasures in states-of-existence (*gati*) either in celestial-region (*svarga*) or among humans (*manuṣya*).

---

20 *saṁsāramatikrānto jīva upādeya iti vicintanīyaḥ* ।
saṁsāraduḥkhākrānto sa heya iti vicintanīyaḥ ॥ — *Bārasa Aṇuvekkhā* 38

21 *aśubhena nirayatiryaṁcyaṁ śubhopabhogena divijanārasaukhyaṁ* ।
śuddhena labhate siddhimevaṁ loko vicintanīyaḥ ॥
— *Bārasa Aṇuvekkhā* 42

> The soul in which manifests the pure cognition (*śuddhopayoga*) attains liberation (*mokṣa*). One should remain engaged in such contemplation on the nature of the universe (*loka*).
>
> —Jain 2021: 74

It is the law of the universe that whoever walks on the path that aligns with the elements and laws of nature, and respects all beings, including oneself, eventually travels from auspicious cognition to pure cognition. Hence, each being has been suggested to focus one's energy on acquiring the right knowledge and right perception, which together lead one towards the upward dimension.

Aśucitva Bhāvanā (Impurity)

Ācārya Kundakunda introduces the aspirant/seeker to perhaps the most bitter truth of life, through this contemplation when he describes:[22]

> The body (*deha, śarīra*) is filled with bile, blood, flesh, fat, bones and marrow; there is abundance of urine, pus and minute worms in it; it is foul-smelling, impure, leathery, ephemeral, inanimate and decaying.
>
> — Ibid.: 82

This teaching seems harsh and disgusting, but we cannot deny its truthfulness. Each of us loves our bodies and loves the form of others through different relationships; however, someone's death shakes us up incredibly when we analyse that the same body has become inanimate now. During that time, we tend to reflect on similar thoughts.

Āsrava Bhāvanā (Influx)

Through our inevitable, incessant activities of ignorance, deluded conduct, soul-soiling emotions of anger, pride, delusion and greed

---

22 *rasarudhiramāṁsamedāsthimajjāsaṅkulaṁ mūtrapūyakrimibahulaṁ* ।
durgandhaṁ aśuci carmamayaṁ anityaṁ acetanaṁ patanaṁ ॥
— *Bārasa Aṇuvekkhā* 45

and the trio of activities of mind, speech and physical actions, we are continuously generating causes and binding future effects for ourselves. Ācārya Kundakunda tells us:[23]

> The soul (*jīva*) has to wander in the world-ocean (*saṁsāra-samudra*) that is full of sea waves, signifying imperfections (like hunger and thirst) and home to water-species (like shark and crocodile), signifying misery, due only to the (kārmic) influx (*āsrava*). —Jain 2021: 96

He shows us the way out and teaches us to recognize the reason of this world and how to get rid of it through these twelve contemplations.

Saṁvara Bhāvanā (Stoppage)

In this reflection, Ācārya Kundakunda throws light upon how right meditation becomes the cause of stoppage of the constant inflow of *karma*, the effect of which, eventually, is liberation,[24]

> through pure cognition (*śuddhopayoga*) the two types of (auspicious) meditation (*dhyāna*) — the virtuous (*dharmya*) and the pure (*śukla*) — are affected. Thus, meditation is the cause of stoppage (*saṁvara*) (of kārmic influx). The knowledgeable soul should constantly keep this in mind. — Ibid.: 115

When the aspirant travels beyond the two negative meditations, *ārtta dhyāna* and *raudra dhyāna*, which are the causes to keep the consciousness bound in the cycle of cause and effect. He can attain those meditative states that take him beyond the ocean of misery and grief, and into its real nature of eternal peace and bliss.

---

23 *āsravahetor jīvo janmasamudre nimajjate kṣipraṁ* ।
āsravakriyā tasmān mokṣanimittaṁ na cintanīyā ॥
— *Bārasa Aṇuvekkhā* 58

24 *śuddhopayogena punar dharmaṁ śuklaṁ ca bhavati jīvasya* ।
tasmāt saṁvarahetu dhyānamiti vicintyen nityam ॥ — Ibid. 64

Nirjarā Bhāvanā (Dissociation)

Shedding the accumulated *karma* happens on its own (with time) or wilfully (with effort). Ācārya Kundakunda clarifies this process in a scientific manner:[25]

> Lord Jina has expounded that putrefaction of the kārmic bondage in the (soul's) space-points (*pradeśa*) is dissociation. Further, know that whatever results in the stoppage (*saṁvara*) also results in the dissociation (*nirjarā*). —Jain 2021: 130

Basically, closing the door (*saṁvara*) not only prevents unwanted *karma* from entering the space points of the soul but is also the cause of realizing the separateness of the opposite nature of consciousness and kārmic particles. Hence, stoppage and dissociation are both the results of the same effect.

Dharma-svākhyātatva Bhāvanā (The Truth Proclaimed by Religion)

The beauty of this reflection, and for that matter, of all twelve reflections, is that the aspirant is not suggested to bow in front of any Supreme Being to please him or get his wishes fulfilled. Rather, one is suggested to dive within to know one's real essence, one is real nature, and should strive to access that. Especially in this reflection, one is advised to augment the traits that strengthen the path towards enlightenment.

> The faith promulgated by Lord Jina has non-injury (*ahiṁsā*) as its mark, truthfulness (*satya*) as its base, humility (*vinaya*) as its root, and forbearance (*kṣamā*) as its strength. It is safeguarded by celibacy (*brahmacarya*), dominated by quietism (*upaśama*), characterized by restraint (*niyati*) and supported by non-attachment (*aparigraha*). — Ibid.: 155

---

25 *bandhapradeśagalanaṁ nirjaraṇaṁ iti hi jinavaropāttaṁ* ।
yena bhavet saṁvaraṇaṁ tena tu nirjaraṇamiti jānīhi ॥
— *Bārasa Aṇuvekkhā* 66

The seeker is advised to polish all these traits from within. He can do so by following those who have already walked on this path before him and laid the foundation.

Bodhi-durlabha Bhāvanā (Rarity of Enlightenment)

In this contemplation, Ācārya Kundakunda emphasizes the rarity of attaining the right knowledge that teaches one to differentiate between what is worth accepting and what is worth rejecting:[26]

> To contemplate on the means that result in acquisition of right-knowledge (*samyag-jñāna*) is the (contemplation of) enlightenment (*bodhi*). This *bodhi* is extremely rare (as a corollary, to acquire right-knowledge is extremely rare). —Jain 2021: 172

Everyone asserts the importance of knowledge for spiritual upliftment, but rarely does someone tell a seeker that the knowledge should also be right. For example, when it comes to religion, we mostly observe the quest to please a higher deity and to pray to them to bless the aspirant. The rarity is to become independent and take absolute charge of one's spiritual journey; in the real sense, this is the purpose of religion.

Hence, we analyse that be it meditation or the twelve contemplations, the philosophy of Jainism prepares the aspirant/seeker to peep within to find one's natural essence, which is beyond the conditioning of the society and of the world, beyond the ambit of senses and the mind, and even beyond the boundaries of a specific religion. That readies the aspirant to have a glimpse into peace and divinity, and to embark on the journey to know thyself and, through that, achieve Godhood (liberation).

Liberation (Mokṣa) and Godhood

If only a guide could direct one in taking charge of one's own rise

---

26 *utpadyate sajjñānaṁ yenopāyena tasyopāyasya* ।
cintā bhavati bodhir atyantaṁ durlabhā bhavati ॥
— *Bārasa Aṇuvekkhā* 83

and fall, God stands at the top rung of the evolutionary ladder and illuminates the same path for all.

Every religion focuses on "God's relationship to the cosmos" (Audi 2010: 815), whether seeing him as the creator and sustainer of the universe or as an individual who has travelled from being a mundane soul to becoming the Absolute Soul (*Paramātmā*), and is now located at the crown of the universe. The Jaina religion supports the latter belief as it

> does not accept the concept of a god who created the universe and who, for that reason, wields a kind of authority to which whole of his creation, including people, must submit itself.
>
> — Zydenbos 2006: 20

Jainism defines God as "soul that is devoid of the slur of the karma is *Paramātmā*" (Varni 2014b: 19). This opens up a gateway of possibilities that raises queries like: As each living being is a manifestation of the soul, does that mean everyone can attain Godhood? If there is no life-giving, sustainer and destructor God, does that mean one is responsible for one's own freedom? Eventually, these queries prepare one to take charge of one's own journey, which is what all Indian philosophies inculcate in the seeker of reality.

Specifically talking about Jaina philosophy,

> Jainism is not a belief system, but rather a way of right relationship with the living universe that we are inherently part of. It is not based upon a theology of a Creator that we must all bow down to, but upon recognition of the sacred nature of all life. — Mardia and Rankin 2013: 1

And getting in absolute sync with the same.

God or Godhood?

Each liberated soul is God
God is that who is liberated.

If one were asked, "Would you like to become God and be the controller of people's destinies, to be able to fulfil their wishes, to curse someone, or to help one attain divinity?", a normal person would reply, "Why would I wish to be stuck in other people's affairs? I have plenty of my own problems". A spiritual person would reply, you are defining God wrong, my friend; how could God "want" in the first place, as he appears to be beyond any desire? Hence, no question arises to be the controller. Also, if God would have created or controlled this universe and its happenings, he would have created a perfect world. However, God can be the one who knows with absolute clarity about how things work. Why there is joy and sorrow in the world? And once he knows it all, why would he still choose to be indulged in the same? He would shun it all and would focus on peeping within.

Absolute freedom is Godhood in the real sense; it means travelling beyond the cycle of cause and effect through real knowledge and attaining the state of zero kārmic baggage. Transtheistic is a term coined by German Indodologist Heinrich Zimmer.

> Zimmer applies the term to the theological system of Jainism, which is theistic in the limited sense that gods exist, but become immaterial as they are transcended by *mokṣa*.[27]
>
> In most living religions today, the emotional side of man is emphasized: faith is demanded more than understanding and this faith should inspire the believer to lead his or her life in a way that finds favour with a higher entity that will decide about the believer's fate in this life as well as in the existence to come.
>
> — Zydenbos 2006: 37

Surrendering to someone, considering him higher than oneself, so much so that he can decide one's fate, seems illogical to a rational mind, for it is tough to surrender to a higher power that will judge

---

[27] "Transtheism", Definitions, 2022, <https://www.definitions.net/definition/transtheism> (accessed on 1 July 2022).

one for each of one's actions. This Indian philosophy conveys that the seeker is free at his will and not answerable to any supernatural being but to himself.

> Jainism is not theistic, hence the question of following the commandments of a divinity does not arise. —Zydenbos 2006: 37

The supreme power lies in one's soul. Though one can follow the footsteps of those who have walked the path of spiritual evolution before him, even they can only show him the way; they cannot do more. At first, statements like these fill one with amazement and fear. Since the day of our birth, we have been taught to fear some supernatural being who lives high up in the skies, noticing and observing even the tiniest of our actions, judging us and, in turn, bearing fruit in the near or distant future. Most people spend their lives in sheer fear of that Supreme Deity. This fear does good, too, as people keep themselves in check and choose to be ethical in their personal and professional dealings. However, as soon as one grows up and starts having a critical and analytical mind, one seems dissatisfied with the above description of God because it eventually puts one in even more dilemmas when one seeks answers to questions like: Who created God? Why does God not want a perfect world? Why is there so much suffering around?, and there are plenty of such unanswered queries.

Arhanta: the crest of evolution

> *Oh soul! Will you stay bound in this cycle forever,*
> *or is there an end?*
> *Of course, with my honest endeavour, I can transcend.*

The state of *arhanta* is also known as *sayoga-kevalī*, when a being reaches the second-to-last rung on the ladder of evolution, the thirteenth *guṇasthāna* (see *Guṇasthānas*). The path of knowledge is to know oneself in absoluteness, as the soul is absolute knowledge and world view. As soon as a normal being starts to peel off the layers of ignorance and wrong beliefs, he starts his journey towards spiritual evolution, which eventually leads to physical evolution. When one reaches a level where one is able to realize everything in its totality, with all its dimensions, in all modes of existence, through all points of view, one becomes efficient at distinguishing between reality and illusion. One becomes equipped to differentiate between the soul and the non-soul. This knowledge initiates the process of shedding immense kārmic layers, with which one has been bound since time immemorial.

According to Jaina philosophy, an individual becomes God after the complete destruction of *karma*. This state of God has two aspects:

> One is the liberated being with the body, and the other is the liberated being without the body. The first stage is called *arhanta,* and the latter is called *siddha.* — Varni 2012: 136

Arhanta (omniscient) is the state of *sayoga-kevalī* (thirteenth *guṇasthāna*) and *siddha* is the stage just after *ayoga-kevalī* (fourteenth *guṇasthāna*). Hence, we see that the state of the *ayoga-kevalī* is the state of "omniscient without *yoga*" and it is only a halt for

> as much time as is required to pronounce five short vowels. At the end of this period the soul leaves the embodied state forever and goes straight above, to the end of the universe, to enjoy its inherent blissfulness forever. — Bhargava 2020: 442

Despite being *arhanta* (the supreme manifestation of being human), the soul is still left with eighty-five *karma prakṛtis* to be destroyed; hence, it is called *sayoga-kevalī* and the moment it sheds these *karma prakṛtis*, it attains the state of the *siddha*. However, in the *Dhavalā*, it has been mentioned:

> *Sayoga-kevalī* and *ayoga-kevalī* both can be called *arhanta* as both have destroyed the destructible *karma* (*ghātīya karma*) and have observed the substances in their absolute completeness through omniscience. — Varni 2012: 138

Till the being is bound in physical form, even till the state of *arhanta*, even when it has stopped the use of three mediums of cause-creating faculties, i.e. mind, speech and actions, it is yet to get rid of the *yoga* that initiates the activities at the first place and acts as an instrument to occupy the other three physical entities. That *yoga* is defined as "vibrations of soul *pradeśa* associated with physical, mental and vocal activities" (Aggarwal 2014: 151). Hence, even the omniscient is called *sayoga-kevalī*, which means "omniscient with *yoga*".

Accessibility of achieving the state of godhood: The Siddha

A state of absolute freedom, where the consciousness is in its purest form, is absolute knowledge and world view. Those who attain this state are known as *siddhas*. *Siddhas*,

> those who have destroyed the restriction of all eight types of *karma*, and are located at the topmost realm of the universe, are absolute and eternal. — Varni 2014b: 323

It is the state where the soul breaks free from the boundaries of physicality and gets itself located at the topmost realm of the universe. Another beauty of Jaina philosophy is that it conveys with absolute surety that each soul is worthy to attain the state of a *siddha*, the state of Godhood, as there are not one or a few *siddhas*, but they, too, are infinite in number. Infinite beings have attained salvation since time immemorial and infinite will continue to achieve this state following the path of right knowledge, right world view and right conduct. It is simple yet profound that whoever pursues the right path will be liberated.

The state of zero *karma* is *mokṣa* and whoever attains this state is the *siddha*. This way, evolution is the journey of becoming *Paramātmā* from *ātmā*.

Tīrthaṁkara: men with exceptional leadership skills

Tīrthaṁkaras are

> great men who not only traverse the ocean of the universe (world) themselves but also guide others to cross over the same.
> — Varni 2014a: 371

However, one prime minister in each country does not mean that no other leaders are present with the same ability. In the scenario of the *tīrthaṁkaras*, they have unique leadership abilities. This does not mean that only they can achieve Godhood (*mokṣa*). "The *tīrthaṁkaras* are not lawmakers but rather the discoverers of eternal laws" (Zydenbos 2006: 21). These laws can be searched by anyone through the trio of right world view, right knowledge and right conduct. These laws are not set by any Supreme Being but are natural and in absolute sync with the universe.

In the text on reality Ācārya Umāsvāti mentions:[28]

> The enlightened world view, enlightened knowledge and enlightened conduct are the path to liberation. — Tatia 2011: 5

This trio is the path to liberation; each step requires innate honesty, purity of intent and extreme self-vigilance to stay on track without deviation. Above all, this vision has to be realized from within and can, in no way, be imposed on the aspirant. It is about accessing the objective truth, the absolute reality with infinite layers of relativity; hence, the doors for scrutiny are open to anyone with a rational and intuitive mind.

> Just as the findings of science are essentially open to verification by anyone who wishes to do so, the truth of the teachings of the *tīrthaṁkaras* can also be realized experientially by anyone.
> — Zydenbos 2006: 21

The journey of seeking the truth belongs to the individual, only he has to take charge. The *tīrthaṁkaras* and the other souls on the path to liberation can only mend their path of knowledge and, in turn, show the way to others, but each seeker of reality has to walk on that path on his own.

Mokṣa (liberation) and the path to attain it

> The summit of evolution for each being is to step out of the cycle of cause and effect, which is *mokṣa*, the soul in its purest state.

---

[28] *samyag-darśana-jñāna-cāritrāṇi mokṣamārgaḥ* । — *Tattvārthasūtra* 1.1

Those who attained liberation conveyed that knowledge to their disciples before their final release. However, no one can define how it feels in that state. But through one's trust, intuition and perception, one gets a glimpse that there lies an eternal, unchangeable state, accessible and achievable by all, that is beyond all baggage, sheer knowledgeable, blissful, and that is *mokṣa*. Varni defines *mokṣa* as:

> Absolute resignation from the eight *karma*s through walking on the path of the trio of enlightened world view, enlightened knowledge and enlightened conduct is substantial liberation (*dravya-mokṣa*) and absolute riddance from feelings of attachment and aversion is spiritual liberation (*bhāva mokṣa*). —2014b: 321

He clarifies further:

> To accomplish a state where the soul absolutely eradicates *bhāva karma* (the psychic dispositions) is *bhāva mokṣa*, and *bhāva mokṣa* enacts as an instrument to initiate the absolute separation of the space-points of soul and *karma*, which is *dravya mokṣa* (substantial liberation). —Ibid.: 323

Even in our day-to-day chores, we observe that everything we do, the idea of it, originates in thoughts first, which later get reflected in physicality. Thoughts that are either of attachment towards a certain work, person, event, destination or of aversion towards a specific work, person, event, destination are possible due to the psychic dispositions (*bhāva-karma*) of the soul. Hence, psychic dispositions act as instrumental causes to generate thoughts, which, in turn, act as the instrumental cause to get the work done physically. This phenomenon works for every occurrence in the universe, be it an underdeveloped being who searches for food or shelter or a being who attains liberation. Hence, we conclude that liberation from psychic dispositions occurs before physical liberation.

> Wake up, O human! Realize thy absolute essence and be free.

There is a final destination, a realization of that destination and a path to that destination. As we have seen previously, the enlightened world view, enlightened knowledge and enlightened conduct consist the path to liberation.

This path is not related to a specific religion or philosophy; it is universal and equally accessible. Not only that, but this path is also not of faith in a Supreme Deity but of sheer independence as "each individual *jīva* has the potential to rise to a state of pure reason and knowledge" (Mardia and Rankin 2013: 79). This way, Jaina philosophy motivates the beings to recognize their essence in their absoluteness.

Now, the question arises: What prevents the soul from walking on the path to liberation? Why does not each soul walk on that path and achieve *mokṣa*? The answer is *karma*[29] and, hence, "the elimination of all types of *karma* is liberation" (Tatia 2011: 254). Ācārya Umāsvāti mentions:[30]

> When all the kārmic bondage is eliminated, the soul soars upward to the border of cosmic space. — Tatia 2011: 255

This solution gives rise to another query: why does the soul soar upward only and not in any other direction? Ācārya Umāsvāti leaves no stone unturned as he clarifies further,[31] "the soul soars up by virtue of its innate mode of upward flight" (Tatia 2011: 255). Varni also states: "upward movement is the natural movement of the soul" (2014a: 235). Liberation is a state; to attain that the soul travels from the practical path (*vyavahāra mārga*) to the transcendental path (*niścaya mārga*). Dayanand Bhargava (2020: 191) writes:

> The ultimate aim is to uproot even the subtlest form of passions.

---

29 *kṛtsnakarmakṣayomokṣaḥ* । — *Tattvārthasūtra* 10.3

30 *tadanataramūrdhvaṁ gacchatyālokāntāt* । — Ibid. 10.5

31 *tathāgati pariṇāmācca* । — Ibid. 10.6

> Therefore, the relative life of vice and virtue is to be abandoned in favour of a life of pure consciousness (*śuddhopayoga*).

As pure consciousness leads to lighter kārmic baggage and the layers of *karma* keep getting shed, the soul starts to shine in its true nature, knowledge and world view.

Mokṣa: A state OF sheer INDEPENDENCE

Whether in our personal or professional lives, we notice a pattern of favouring each other to coexist peacefully. One helps the other with their unique talents and, in turn, either earns finances or gets some other favour from the one helped. Similarly, Jainism puts even the deities into the category of giving and getting favour in return. One can please a particular deity through worshipping, fasting, offering sacrifices, etc., which in turn indicates vices of attachment and aversion even in the deities. This way, we analyse that even the heavenly beings are *karma*-bound. Hence, "Jainism does not accept the idea of imperfect deities as controlling forces" (Mardia and Rankin 2013: 79) of neither one's fate nor any other occurrence in the universe.

However, to attain liberation, a being travels from relativity to absolutism. Each religious philosophy depicts a path of relativity; once the soul crosses over a certain stage of the same, it rises above relativity and, hence, crosses the boundaries of religion. In Jainism, this is the ninth rung on the ladder of spiritual evolution (see *Guṇasthāna*), where the soul "rises above religion and attains true humanity" (Jain 2014: 118) or the crest of evolution.

It is achievable by anyone, has been achieved by many in the past and will be achieved by many in future. Just like many roads can lead to the same destination, there are many roads to enlightenment.

Bibliography

Primary Sources

Bārasa Aṇuvettā, Ācārya Kundakunda.

Pañcāstikāya, Ācārya Kundakunda.

Samaṇa Suttam.

Samayasāra, Ācārya Kundakunda.

Tattvārthasūtra, Ācārya Umāsvāti.

Tiloyapaṇṇatti, Vrishabhacharya Yati.

Secondary Sources

Aggarwal, Paras Mal, 2014, *Soul Science: Samayasāra by Jain Ācārya Kundakunda*, Indore: Kundakunda Gyānapītha.

Audi, Robert (ed.), 2017/2015/2010, *The Cambridge Dictionary of Philosophy*, New York: Cambridge University Press.

Basu, Major B.D., 1915, *Sāṁkhya Philosophy*, Sacred Books of the Hindus, vol. 11, Allahabad: The Panini Office.

Bhandari, Narendra, 2015, *Jainism: The Eternal and Universal Path to Enlightenment — A Scientific Synthesis*, Jaipur: Prakrit Bharati Academy.

Bhandari, Narendra and Surendra Singh Pokharna, 2017, *Syādavāda and Anekāntavāda in the Modern Scientific Context: Scientific Perspectives of Jainism*, BMIRC Monograph Series, Ladnun, Rajasthan: Jain Vishva Bharati Institute.

Bhargava, Dayanand, 2020, *Samaṇa Suttaṁ: Essence of Jainism*, Jaipur: Hansa Prakashan.

Bhattacharya, Shantanu, 2021, "Sage who dreamed of the atom", Santanub. medium.com.

Bhatnagar, M.S., 1984, Atom from Vedas to Date", *Indian Journal of History of Science*, 19(4): 323-28.

Bollée, Willem, 2010, *Samantabhadra Deva's Ratnakaraṇḍakaśrāvakācāra*, Bangalore: Sundar Prakashan.

Flügel, Peter (ed.), 2014, *International Journal of Jaina Studies*, vols 7-9, Mumbai: Hindi Granth Karyalaya.

Grover, Harpreet Singh, 2020, "Of the People, By the People, For the People", *Journal of Indian Society of Periodontology*, 24(3): 190 NCBI, May-June, <https://www.ncbi.nlm.nih.gov/pmc/articles/PMC7307473/> (accessed on 8 January 2022).

Hoyle, Fred, 1955, *Frontiers of Astronomy*, Heinemann Education Books Archive. org. <https://archive.org/details/frontiersofastro031522mbp/page/n357/mode/2up> (accessed on 8 October 2021).

Jain, Amit, 2014, *Guide to Godhood: The Roadmap to Moksha* (*Based on Shramanasutram*), New Delhi: Munshiram Manoharlal.

Jain, Vijay K. (ed. and tr.), 1994, *Ācārya Kundakunda's Samayasāra*, New Delhi: Kundakunda Bharati.

Jain, Medhavi, 2020, "Zero and Infinity in Mathematics: Ayoga Kevalī and Siddha in Jain Philosophy", *ISJS Transaction* (January–March), 5(15).

Jain, Vijay K. (ed. and tr.), 2020, *Pañcāstikāya-Saṁgraha: The Jaina Metaphyscis*, Dehradun: Vikalp Printers.

——, 2021, *Bārasa Aṇuvekkhā: The Twelve Contemplations*, Dehradun: Vikalp Printers.

Jalaj, Jaikumar (tr.), 2016, *Ācārya Kundakunda's Pañcāstikāya*, Kota: Paras Mool Chand Chatar Charitable Trust.

Jha, Alok, 2013, "What Is Heisenberg's Uncertainty Principle?" (10 November), Theguardian.com, <https://www.theguardian.com/science/2013/nov/10/what-is-heisenbergs-uncertainty-principle> (accessed on 29 July 2021).

Jung, C.G., 2006, *The Undiscovered Self*, New York: New American Library, Penguin Group.

Kachchara, Narayan Lal, 2011, "Philosophy of Mind: A Jain Perspective", spiritualsciencesg.com, <https://spiritualsciencesg.com/book-article/nl17.pdf> (accessed on 12 April 2022).

——, 2014, *Scientific Explorations of Jain Doctrines* (Part 1), Delhi: Motilal Banarsidass.

Kaku, Michio and Jennifer Thompson, 1995, *Beyond Einstein: The Cosmic Quest for the Theory of the Universe*, New York: Anchor Books.

Latash, Mark and L. Zatsiorsky, 2016, "M. Reflexes", sciencedirect.com, <https://www.sciencedirect.com/topics/neuroscience/reflex> (accessed on 5 April 2022).

Mahaprajna, Acharya, 2003, *The Quest for Truth: In Context of Anekanta*, Ladnun, Rajasthan: Jain Vishva Bharati Institute.

——, 2010, *Abstract Thinking*, Ladnun, Rajasthan: Jain Vishva Bharati Institute.

——, 2013, *Mind Beyond Mind*, Delhi: Adarsh Sahitya Sangh.

Mahendra Kumar (Muni) 2010, *The Enigma of the Universe*, Ladnun, Rajasthan: Jain Vishva Bharati Institute.

Malhotra, Nishi, 2015, "20 Greatest World Leaders and Thinkers Who Were Inspired by Mahatma Gandhi", 2 October 2015 (accessed on 23 January 2021). <https://www.thebetterindia.com/35422/20-greatest-world-leaders-and-thinkers-who-were-inspired-by-mahatma-gandhi/>

Mallo, John, 2015, "Commentary: Millions Have Died in the Name of Religion" (3 December), swnewsmedia.com. SW News Media 2022. <https://www.swnewsmedia.com/eden_prairie_news/news/opinion/guest_columns/commentary-millions-have-died-in-the-name-of-religion/article_8f8ee092-5810-5d3d-9be6-f7fa277a0700.html>

Mardia, Kanti V. and Aidan D. Rankin, 2013, *Living Jainism: An Ethical Science*, London: Mantra Books.

Mishra, Ashok K., 2006, "Atomism of Nyāya-Vaiśeṣika vs. Jainism: A Scientific Appraisal", *Indian Journal of History of Science*, 41.3: 247-61.

Moskowitz, Clara, 2011, "What's 96 Per Cent of the Universe Made of?", space.com (12 May), <https://www.space.com/11642-dark-matter-dark-energy-4-per cent-universe-panek.html> (accessed on 24 March 2021).

Rand, Ayn, 1952, *The Fountainhead*, New York: New American Library, A Division of Penguin Group, USA.

Ricee, Susanne, 2021, "Subconscious vs Unconscious: The Complete Comparison", diversity.social, 26 May, <https://diversity.social/unconscious-vs-subconscious/> (accessed on 7 April 2022).

Schaeffer, Asa A., 1917, "Reactions of Amoeba to Light and the Effect of Light on Feeding", *Biological Bulletin*, 32(2), The University of Chicago Press Journals, 1917: 61 <https://www.jstor.org/stable/pdf/1536417.pdf> (accessed on 3 January 2022).

Shri Yati Vrishabhacharya (tr)., 2006, *Aryika Vishuddhamati*, tr. ed. Chetanprakash Patni, *Tiloypaṇṇatti* 2, Acharya Bahubali Adhyatmik Anusandhan trust, Shikohpur, Gurgaon, p.

Schubring, Walther, 2000, *The Doctrine of the Jainas*, Delhi: Motilal Banarsidass.

Scott, Elizabeth, 2020, "What Is the Law of Attraction" (18 November), <https://www.verywellmind.com/understanding-and-using-the-law-of-attraction-3144808> (accessed on 25 January 2021).

Siegel, Ethan, 2019, "This Is Why Time Has to Be a Dimension", Forbes.com, 27 August, <https://www.forbes.com/sites/startswithabang/2019/08/27/this-is-why-time-has-to-be-a-dimension/?sh=788dcd233646> (accessed on 31 August 2021).

Sikdar, J.C., 1978, *Indian Concepts of Matter*, part 1, Ahmedabad: L.D. Institute of Indology.

Sogani, Kamal Chand, 2001, *Ethical Doctrines in Jainism*, Solapur: Jaina Samskriti Samrakshak Sangha.

Stafford, Tom, 2015, "Your subconscious is smarter than you might think", bbc.com, 18 February 2015, <https://www.bbc.com/future/article/20150217-how-smart-is-your-subconscious> (accessed on 5 April 2022).

Tater, Sohan Raj, 2009, *The Jaina Doctrine of Karma and the Science of Genetics*, New Delhi: Readworthy Publications.

Tatia, Nathmal (ed. & tr.), 2011, *Tattvārtha Sūtra: That Which Is*, New Haven and London: Yale University Press.

Thornton, Philip K., 2010, "Livestock Production: Recent Trends, Future Prospects", *Phil. Trans. R. Soc.*, B27 365 (1554): 2053-67. <https://royalsocietypublishing.org/doi/10.1098/rstb.2010.0134> (accessed on 31 August 2022).

Tobias, Michael, 1991, *Life Force: The World of Jainism*, Fremont, CA: Jain Publishing Company.

Tolle, Eckhart, 2001, *The Power of Now*, Mumbai: Yogi Impressions.

Tripathi, Amish, 2010, *The Immortals of Meluha*, Chennai: Westland.

——, 2011, *The Secret of the Nagas*, Chennai: Westland.

Varni, Jinendra, 2012, *Jainendra Siddhānta Kośa*, vol. 1, New Delhi: Bharatiya Jnanpith.

——, 2014a, *Jainendra Siddhānta Kośa*, vol. 2, New Delhi: Bharatiya Jnanpith.

——, 2014b, *Jainendra Siddhānta Kośa*, vol. 3, New Delhi: Bharatiya Jnanpith.

Vrishabhacharya, Yati, and Aryika Vishuddhamati, 2006, *Tiloypannatti*, tr. Chetan Prakash Patni, ed. Shikohpur, Gurgaon: Acharya Bahubali Adhyatmik Anusandhan Trust.

Weiss, Brian, 2000, *Messages from the Masters*, Chatham, UK: CPI Mackays.

Weiss, L. Brian, 2010, *Messages from the Masters*, London: Piatkus.

Williams, R., 1998, *Jaina Yoga*, Delhi: Motilal Banarsidass.

Zydenbos, Robert, 2006, *Jainism Today and Its Future* (PDF), München: Manya Verlag.

Websites

https://santanub.medium.com

https://en.wikipedia.org

https://ia902705.us.archive.org

https://plato.stanford.edu

www.britannica.com

www.pbs.org

www.sciencefocus.com

www.youtube.com

Index